LINCOLN CHRISTIAN ___ W9-CCW-338

Two in the Pulpit

Thomas H. Conley

Two in the Pulpit

Sermons in Dialogue

WORD BOOKS, PUBLISHER
WACO, TEXAS

TWO IN THE PULPIT

Copyright © 1973 by Word, Incorporated
Waco, Texas 76703

All rights reserved.
No part of this book may be reproduced
or transmitted in any form or by any means,
electronic or mechanical, including photocopying,
recording, or by any information storage and
retrieval system, except for brief
quotations in reviews, without
written permission from
the publisher.

Library of Congress catalog card number: 72–96360
Printed in the United States of America

All New Testament quotations are from the Today's English Version of
the New Testament. Copyright © American Bible Society 1966. Used by
permission. Quotations marked RSV are from the Revised Standard Version of the Bible, copyright 1946 and 1952 by the Division of Christian
Education of the National Council of Churches of Christ in the United
States of America, and are used by permission. Quotation marked KJV is
from the Authorized Version of the Bible, commonly called the King
James Version.

To
E. R. Bishop, my father-in-law,
whose dialogue in life was of love and grace

130534

Acknowledgments

I once ended a poem about three of my many selves:

> I am the seasons, the winds, the
>   numbers of clustered stars.
> I want them all, and sometimes none.
> I shall die with part of all,
>   and all of some,
> But none totally me.

In the same sense, these dialogue sermons are "part of all, and all of some, but none totally me." I am indebted to my teachers at Southern Baptist Theological Seminary who enlarged my horizons and tapped my creativity: Dr. James Cox, my teacher in Christian preaching, and the now deceased Dr. Harold Cooke Phillips, guest lecturer for a time in Christian preaching at Southern; Dr. Wayne E. Oates, my supervisory professor in my Th.M. work; Dr. Samuel Southard, friend and major professor until a sabbatical interrupted; and Dr. Charles A. McGlon, speech and drama professor at Southern Seminary, who encouraged me to send my work for publication.

Floyd Thatcher, executive editor of Word Books, made helpful suggestions as to refinement and style, and without his interest this book could never be. Dr. John Carlton, professor of preaching at Duke University Divinity School and Southeastern Baptist Theological Seminary, gave encouragement and help.

My appreciation goes also to Lucille Pickett, my secretary, who painstakingly typed and retyped the manuscript and never lost her sense of humor and willingness. My congregation has listened, interacted, and allowed me the freedom necessary for the discipline of writing. To them I am grateful.

To those whose ideas have become such a part of me that I cannot now differentiate between theirs and mine, and whose thoughts appear somewhere in the dialogues—accept this as credit and appreciation for your inspiration and thoughts.

Finally, my family has been patient and has given encouragement even when my writing took time and energy from them. To my wife, Betty, and our two boys, Scott and Sean, go unending love and appreciation for their affection and succor.

Contents

The pulpit is ever the earth's foremost part. . . . The world's a ship on its passage out . . . and the pulpit is its prow.[1]

The Dialogue Sermon: An Introduction

This is an age of renewal and re-formation in the Church. Bristling winds of change and resurgence have been blowing through stained glass windows and stirring to new life the dry, dead bones of a tradition-encrusted Christianity. These winds have not come too soon. Reinhold Niebuhr, as far back as 1924, saw the need for renewal.

> The church has lost the chance of becoming the unifying element in our American society. It is not anticipating any facts. It is merely catching up and very slowly to the new social facts created by economic and other forces. . . . We are not creating. We are merely catching up with creation.[2]

What Niebuhr suspected when he wrote these words as a young minister in Detroit, Michigan, has become true for the now-urbanized America and its Christian Church.

Organized religion is faring well today in terms of its great numbers of people. It is another story in the influence exercised by institutional Christianity. Edmund Steimle has asked,

. . . in hiring and firing, buying and selling, taking a job or turning it down, in voting booths or in those private chambers of the safety deposit vaults at the local bank, how often do you think, does Christian commitment seriously affect those daily decisions?[3]

This book is written out of the belief that one of the reasons the Church is in trouble is because of the failure of preaching, the *Empty Pulpit*, as Clyde Reid has called it.[4] Reid makes a significant point when he observes that this is not an absolute emptiness, but it is emptiness, nevertheless.[5] The "new reformation" of the twentieth century brings hope not only to the pulpit, but to the Church as well.

Hendrik Kraemer feels that the reformation of today will have more impact than the reformation of the sixteenth century. The "pressure both of the Spirit and of the world are upon us to rethink and reshape the response of the divine calling of the Church."[6]

The heart and soul of the worshiping church is its proclamation, the *kerygma*, the message of what God has done and is doing in His world. Therefore, if there is something lacking in the presentation of the *kerygma*, there will be a deficiency in the Church. Much of the trouble with the Church is the trouble with preaching. Pierre Berton, a Canadian author, has described many sermons heard by the laity as "spiritless, irrelevant, dull, and badly delivered."[7] This writer believes Berton has correctly described much of Christian preaching today. If there is to be renewal in the Church, there must also be renewal in the pulpit.

There will be some who fail to take seriously the criticism leveled at the "empty pulpit." But it is difficult to ignore the stern warning of a preacher like Helmut Thielicke, for years in the pulpit at St. Michael's in Hamburg, Germany. "Actually preaching itself has decayed and disintegrated to the point where it is close to the stage of dying."[8] He goes on to describe why preaching is decadent. He blames the mere grinding out of a routine vocabulary—

God, grace, sin, justification—which produces a kind of Christian gobbledegook that never gets under anybody's skin and at most elicits the reaction: Well, that's the way the minister *has* to speak, but what's it to me?[9]

It is evident to many who care about the Church that "business as usual" preaching will not persuade twentieth century men and women of anything. This age is perhaps the most ambivalent of man's tenure on earth. A running catalogue on the condition of modern man tells us that he is organized, challenged, surfeited, manipulated, adjusted, alienated, exhilarated, depressed, inspired, contended, robotized, silent, and prosperous.

Conventional preaching has all too often failed to come to grips with truth and reality in the blood-and-guts world where people live. Thielicke has sensed this.

> The safest advice to give to the man who wants to get through unscathed is to tell him to stick to conventional preaching. Boresomeness paralyzes people, but it does not make them angry. . . . Nobody is ever shocked by lukewarm drip from the pulpit. . . .[10]

There is little place for the preacher who desires to soft-pedal the issues; push aside the social demands of a twentieth century world, and relegate to others painful decisions on the hard questions of the hour. Reinhold Niebuhr knew the truth: "Innocuous virtue is always more charming and more liable to prompt a generous affection than the kind which raises disquieting questions."[11]

The dialogue sermon is not a panacea for either all the ills of the Church, or all the emptiness of the modern pulpit. But if used effectively, it can breathe some new life into preaching. It has the potentiality of stimulating the mind, expanding the imagination, and involving the listener in the truth being presented.

There are several essential marks in the preparation of the dialogue sermon. There must first be a principal idea that the preacher wishes to communicate. This idea may be generated by the study of Scripture, a situation recorded in the newspaper, or a personal experience that has spiritual truth. The presentation of a central idea is not unlike preparation for any sermon. There must be a theme, a thesis, a proposition to be given to the people.

The dialogue sermon must be prepared so that the ideas presented in the message are consistent with scriptural truth. There are times when a character in the dialogue can phrase a biblical truth so uniquely that it tends to "hang" in the listener's mind. However the truth is put, it must be scripturally sound.

The third ingredient in the dialogue sermon is imagination. In a specific situation what might these persons have said to one another? For example, Job's wife tells him to "curse God and die." But in all probability, there were additional exchanges between them. This summary of his wife's attitude must have been surrounded by more dialogue than we have. Given the situation, the dramatic milieu, his wife's chagrin, and Job's faith, what could they have said to one another? A dialogue sermon is motivated and molded by imagination. To prepare an effective sermon in dialogue an active imagination is demanded.

Another characteristic in preparation of the dialogue is a sense of history. There is a distinction, however, between a sermon's being "history" or "antihistory." It is valid to have a dialogue not recorded by history as long as it is not opposed to actual history. For example, in the sermon "He's Turned the Tables," there is a dialogue between Nicodemus and Ezra. Now there is no record of this conversation in the Scriptures. There is no evidence that a Jew named Ezra was ever responsive to Jesus or talked with Nicodemus about the Christ. Yet, while this dialogue is not actual history, it is not antihistory. It *could* have happened. Nicodemus was a member of the Sanhedrin. He was interested in Jesus (John 3), and almost certainly discussed Jesus with his colleagues. It is historically feasible that Nicodemus did have a Jewish colleague named Ezra, and that at some time in their relationship they talked about this young prophet, Jesus, who was disturbing their Jewish faith. As long as the sermon is not antihistory and is scripturally sound, its presentation is valid.

The last essential quality is empathy. Empathy means to

"feel with" the persons in the dialogue. Unless the writer of the sermon can put himself into the "skin" of his characters, the lines will be phony and stilted. In the dialogue mentioned above between Nicodemus and Ezra, the writer had to feel the ambivalence of Nicodemus. He wanted to believe in Jesus but was torn between the Christ and his Jewish heritage. Ezra's being threatened by this new religion, this new Kingdom, and his defensiveness against them, had to be felt by the writer. The writer has to "become" the persons he portrays. He must "feel with" them. The preacher must continuously ask: Given the historical setting, the situation that exists between these persons, taking into account the clues to their character given me by the Scriptures and history, what would they do and say?

There may be characters portrayed who are not in the biblical witness at all. These, then, have to become real to the preacher and must act consistently within their historical context. The writer sometimes creates characters, and he must also "feel with" them.

To use this method of preaching effectively, the preacher must take time to explain to his congregation what a dialogue sermon is. The setting of the sermon should be simple. It is best to keep it uncomplicated, especially in the first several dialogues used. Once the congregation has understood the motif of the dialogue sermon they should be able to adapt quickly to its form.

In introducing a given sermon, the preacher should choose a stance for each character. This writer has found that a short step to the left and right of the center of the pulpit, with a slight turn of the body, is enough to convey the difference in characters. It should be emphasized that these are slight turns. The writer has never found it necessary to step from behind the pulpit in presenting a dialogue.

A further aid to the congregation is the inclusion of the name of the person to whom the portrayed character is talking. In the above mentioned sermon between Nicodemus and Ezra the expression, "Let me tell you, Ezra, . . ." immediately identifies the speaker as Nicodemus.

Finally, the preacher must be thoroughly prepared. A manuscript is usually called for. There are times when the preacher can "ad lib" in the dialogue, but when this is done precision and movement are usually sacrificed. This writer uses a full manuscript. However, care should be taken *not* to read the dialogue. Familiarity with the sermon should be such that a glance at the next few lines will trigger the ensuing conversation.

One of the most evident advantages of the dialogue sermon is that it involves the congregation in the action. Their imagination is captured, and most congregations will sit in rapt attention during a dialogue. I recall an eleven-year-old girl in one church. The dialogue had reached an emotional peak where one character was demanding of the other, "Did you mean to say that? Did you mean to do what you did?" The eleven-year-old cried out, "No! No!" That is involvement! With this kind of participation the truths presented are perhaps less likely to be forgotten so quickly.

Another advantage is that preaching is made fresher with this approach. It enables the preacher to get across a familiar biblical truth with a more modern method. The usual sermon is likely to be one through which, in effect, the preacher says to the congregation, "I speak, you listen." The dialogue sermon says to the congregation, "The characters speak, you participate."

The development of the dialogue technique can give the preacher an additional style of presenting the gospel. The expository, topical, life-situation and other functional forms employ essentially the same style. The dialogue technique is different and adds another dimension to the several well-known styles currently used.

Our age is one in which persons see quality on the stage, television, and in the movies. Preaching in the church should not be a come-down in quality, truth, or method of presentation.

There are some disadvantages to the dialogue sermon, too. It is a relatively new method of preaching. Some may feel that this method of preaching is not really "preaching the gospel." These persons can simply be reminded that the *kerygma* is the same, only the method has been changed. Some who are opposed to this method of preaching at first later may come to appreciate it and respond warmly to it. The fact that it is a "new" approach may, however, be a disadvantage at first.

Another limitation to the sermon is inherent in the limitations of the preacher himself. The question has been asked of the writer, "Doesn't a preacher have to be rather dramatic before this kind of sermon can be used?" The answer is that a sense of the dramatic makes the dialogue sermon more effective. It must be done well or it loses its purpose. A poorly done dialogue sermon is perhaps more noticeable than a poorly done sermon of a more orthodox style. However, a preacher should make several attempts at this style before concluding that this is not for him. It should be remembered that this is to be used as an alternative style and method. It is not to replace a preacher's primary styles.

A final disadvantage is that the dialogue probably cannot be used often. It is effective in the congregational involvement it demands, but it seems best to use this style only once every two or three months. This depends of course, on several factors. Can the preacher sustain this high level of creativity and preparation more than once every eight or ten weeks? Can the congregation be pressed into such participation each week? As one woman put it to the writer after a dialogue, "I'm so glad you don't do this often. I get so involved in the dialogue, I'm very tired when you're finished."

There may be other advantages and disadvantages according to the preacher and the congregation. These, however, are the ones encountered by the writer.

NOTES

[1] Herman Melville, *Moby Dick* (New York: Modern Library, 1926), p. 38.

[2] Reinhold Niebuhr, *Leaves from the Notebook of a Tamed Cynic* (Cleveland: The World Publishing Company, 1929), p. 90.

[3] William E. Hulme, *Your Pastor's Problems: A Guide for Ministers and Laymen* (New York: Doubleday & Company, Inc., 1966), p. 161.

[4] Clyde Reid, *The Empty Pulpit: A Study in Preaching As Communication* (Evanston: Harper & Row, Publishers, 1967).

[5] Ibid., p. 9.

[6] Hendrik Kraemer, *A Theology of the Laity* (Philadelphia: The Westminster Press, 1958), p. 99.

[7] Pierre Berton, *The Comfortable Pew* (Philadelphia: J. B. Lippincott Company, 1965), pp. 96–97.

[8] Helmut Thielicke, *The Trouble with the Church*, trans. John W. Doberstein (New York: Harper & Row, Publishers, 1965), p. 2.

[9] Ibid., pp. 2–3.

[10] Ibid., pp. 40–41.

[11] Niebuhr, *op. cit.*, p. 213.

God is not dead to me, but his church is perilously uninvolved in his world. We are wedded to the establishment, prostituted to vested interests, and dedicated to the great leap backwards!

....

If I didn't care, or if I didn't understand what the church is intended to be, it wouldn't matter. But when I see the church of the Master stuck in its own traditional muck, die-hard traditionalism, and rejoicing her mission to the world, I just get angry!—Jeff

The Juniper Tree

And Ahab told Jezebel all that Elijah had done, and withal how he had slain all the prophets with the sword. Then Jezebel sent a messenger unto Elijah, saying, So let the gods do to me, and more also, if I make not thy life as the life of one of them by to-morrow about this time. And when he saw that, he arose, and went for his life, and came to Beersheba, which belongeth to Judah, and left his servant there. But he himself went a day's journey into the wilderness, and came and sat down under a juniper tree: and he requested for himself that he might die; and said, It is enough; now, O Lord, take away my life; for I am not better than my fathers.—*1 Kings 19: 1-4, KJV*

And so I tell you: you are a rock, Peter, and on this rock I will build my church. Not even death will ever be able to overcome it.—*Matthew 16:18*

Frank: Jeff! Jeff! Wait up! Hey, man, how are you?
Jeff: Great, Frank. It's good to see you. Why, it must have been two years since I saw you last.
Frank: No, it's been longer than that. Three at least. It was the convention in Miami, wasn't it?

Jeff: I believe you're right. Three years! Seems impossible. Well, how are you?

Frank: Fine. How are Sue and the boys?

Jeff: She's fine. The boys *and our daughter* are all well.

Frank: A daughter! When?

Jeff: Last year about this time. That's one reason I didn't make it to the convention. By the way, is Frieda all right?

Frank: She's doing well. We have a boy since we've last seen one another. He's a real pistol!

Jeff: I'll bet. Say, we've got a good half hour before the opening session of the convention. Let's find us a nearby restaurant and catch up with one another.

Frank: Right! Old seminary buddies ought to keep up better anyway! Let's go. Say, how's the church getting along?

Jeff: Okay, I guess.

Frank: You guess? What kind of talk is that?

Jeff: I suppose you haven't heard.

Frank: Heard what?

Jeff: I'm out of the pastoral ministry, Frank. As a matter of fact I'm out of the ministry for good. I'm selling insurance for a living now.

Frank: What happened, Jeff? Oh, here's a place, let's get something to drink. Why did you leave the ministry? What happened?

Jeff: Oh, I guess my goals were too high for the church. It seems like we've lost our way, Frank. Oh, I'll take a malted milk shake, please.

Frank: Give me a strawberry soda, please. What do you mean?

Jeff: Well, you know how seriously I've always taken my ministry and the church. To put it in a word, I think the church has sold out to its culture. I think we've accommodated ourselves to the convenience of men instead of following God's direction.

Frank: Well, in a way I can't blame you. I know the feeling. There are men all over the country who have despaired of the ministry and the church. It seems like they're leaving by the hundreds.

Jeff: Since I've been out in the insurance world, I've found a lot of men who were ministers. The unrest in the clergy

that remains is deep and real. At least that's what I've
found.

Frank: I see it, too. It all reminds me of Elijah under the juniper tree, remember? Beset by problems from Ahab and
Jezebel, he felt no one else was with him. So he sat under
the juniper tree and wished he could die. But you know
that story.

Jeff: I have felt for Elijah many times. I know his lament.

Frank: What's wrong, Jeff? Is it the church, the kind of ministers we have? What is the problem?

Jeff: I think it may be both. But with me, most of the problem
lies in the church. There are too many who are unconcerned about the pressing issues of the day. It's almost as
if they were saying, "We're saved; that's all that matters.
We can let the rest of the world go by."

Frank: I know. And the ones that are concerned are frequently
unteachable—not childlike in their faith at all. They've become recalcitrant to innovative or creative ventures.

Jeff: Yes, I used to say that these kinds of persons had bought
them a theological position, like they did their house, forty
years ago, and that's where they'll live till they die!

Frank: And naturally our young, bright, dedicated men are
fearful of this kind of church. I interviewed a young semi-
narian the other day for a youth position in our church.
You know what he told me? I'll see if I can quote him
exactly. "It seems as if the church isn't going anywhere
and won't do anything even if it arrives accidentally."

Jeff: That's about it. God is not dead to me, but his church is
perilously uninvolved in his world. We are wedded to the
establishment, prostituted to vested interests, and dedicated to the great leap backwards!

Frank: Wow! There's still plenty of hostility there!

Jeff: I can't help it, Frank. If I didn't care, or if I didn't understand what the church is intended to be, it wouldn't matter. But when I see the church of the Master stuck in its
own traditional muck, die-hard traditionalism, and rejecting her mission to the world, I just get angry!

Frank: I have felt it, too. There are some who feel comfortable
singing, "When We All Get To Heaven," while people are
living in hell around them.

17

Jeff: You know, Frank, I can take people like this as long as they are teachable, as long as they know something is wrong. But I became weary of feeling that I couldn't teach what I had learned in seminary. I felt like a doctor who knew the diagnosis but could only treat the disease with band-aids, salves, and a gentle bedside manner.

Frank: So rather than sacrifice your integrity . . .

Jeff: [*Interrupts.*] I got out. Right! And the image they expected me to fulfill! Man! I guess some of the pastor's image is valid. But it really began to get to my family when everyone commented on when I took my vacation, how far away from home I went, what kind of mouthwash I used, and how I tied my shoe laces.

Frank: I've often said that if some of our members were as concerned and involved with major problems as they are with trivialities, the church would literally change the world. Racism, poverty, overpopulation, war, economic injustice. These are some of the issues we need to face. Instead we end up fighting each other.

Jeff: I just picked up a new book on the church in the bookstore display at the convention hall. I happened to read one quote in it just before I bought it. It sums up the pressures of the church on a man who tries to speak God's word. Would you like to hear it?

Frank: By all means. Read it.

Jeff: It's how one young preacher feels about a culture-controlled church. "If I preach on war, I will have half a dozen who will tune me out before I get started and another half dozen who will get violent over what I say. I can't preach the biblical injunctives of war and peace. For many in my congregation, there is no word from the Lord on this issue."

Frank: He speaks the truth.

Jeff: There's more. Listen. "If I preach on race, you can be sure the budget receipts will drop for two or three weeks to warn me about the economic reprisals that can come my way. If I preach on poverty, someone will say sarcastically, 'I fight poverty. I work.' They will never understand the deep sociological, economic and spiritual problems here."

18

Frank: Loose him, Lord!

Jeff: [*Continues to read.*] "In short, I am allowed to preach only on community consensus, only on what everyone expects me to say, or what they expect God to condone. I am the caretaker of a religion-in-general, a fashionable, conventional, patriotic folk-faith that fits snugly into the ready-made molds of society and doesn't even know that it has sold out. I run a well-organized church. But I am reminded that graveyards are well organized, too. Only there's no life there, only caretakers."

Frank: Man! He tells it like it is.

Jeff: You mentioned a few minutes ago another reason for unrest in the ministry. As I see it, I became disheartened not only because of the pressures in the church. The men in the pulpit, my colleagues, caused me considerable dismay.

Frank: I have an idea you're about ready to stop cutting the nail and start trimming the flesh!

Jeff: No. Nothing personal, Frank. It's just that I think the church can become the Body of Christ only if her leaders, her prophets, her ministers do their jobs.

Frank: I think I hear you. But be more specific.

Jeff: I believe it was Reinhold Niebuhr who said that the ministry requires "the knowledge of a social scientist and the insight and skill of a poet, the executive talents of a businessman and the mental discipline of a philosopher."[1]

Frank: It was Niebuhr. And he was, and is, correct. Yet, how many men are there like this? Not enough. I know the problem, Jeff. I tug at it every day. There is the task of being husband, father, pastor, counselor, administrator, visitor, prophet, philosopher, and preacher.

Jeff: It's in the call to be prophet where we miss out so often. I've found ten thousand subtle, invisible pressures persuading me not to be prophet. Some of us sell out, that's all. We tell the people what they want to hear instead of what they need to hear.

Frank: And we are paid well for it. It's just like it always has been, Jeff. In Jeremiah's time you'll remember he was run off the temple steps and escaped within an inch of his life. Why? Because the other prophets were crying "Peace, peace," and there was no peace.

19

Jeff: This is really the major issue with me, Frank. Can the church sell out until and unless her prophets have sold out first?

Frank: I don't think so. But it's so easy to remain quiet in a moment of pressure. And there's always the threat of losing your job.

Jeff: Yes, but somehow it always seemed more important for me to do my job than to keep my job.

Frank: Your mention of selling out keeps bringing back memories of something Niebuhr once said about the eunuch gracing his master's establishment, but I can't remember it.

Jeff: Ah, yes. I know it. I have lived with it. He was once describing a man who had sold out to his culture. I'll never forget the quote. "But he seemed to me to be one of those satisfied and complacent chaplains who has fed so long at the flesh-pots of Egypt that he resents anything which disturbs his ease. A man like that reminds me of the eunuchs of old who were robbed of their virility that they might adorn without endangering their masters' luxurious establishments."[2]

Frank: You know, Jeff, ministers have recently been classified as self-employed by the Internal Revenue Service. It's just a thought. Maybe that's our problem: self-employed instead of God-directed!

Jeff: But if a man's going to be God-directed he's going to have to have time to let God through. This means some reflection, meditation, silence.

Frank: And some study. I trust that God can work more quickly and incisively through an informed mind than an empty one. That's one of the problems I see in the colleagues around me. They don't study.

Jeff: I saw this, too. I can remember old Professor Harden lecturing in Christian preaching, his white hair shining in the sunlight and that Scottish accent clipping out that Latin: *maledictus est qui facit opus Dei negligenter.*

Frank: "Young lads," he used to say, "that, roughly translated, means, 'a study that is a lounge makes a pulpit that is an impertinence.'" It's hard to say it better than that.

Jeff: It is, indeed. Yet so many men seem to make a virtue out of ignorance. Sincerity, sanctity, and sobriety are never adequate substitutes for study. I remember reading somewhere that there is a saying on a monastery in Spain that goes: "Nobody gives thanks to a dry stream bed for the water it used to bring."

Frank: Beautifully said. I feel of one mind with you. I know the tugs and pulls as we have talked here. But tell me, Jeff, weren't there any good memories left?

Jeff: By all means. I had an indescribable feeling when I had saved a marriage with my little know-how in pastoral care. It was fulfilling to go back into that home and hear laughter in the walls again.

Frank: Yes. I know the feeling.

Jeff: Or, watch someone grow closer to the Kingdom. It thrilled me to see the light dawn, the fog lift about a new idea and one of my people become involved in a fresh experience with Christ.

Frank: That's hard to beat.

Jeff: I remember my joy at seeing a couple have their first child after twelve years of marriage. I was as happy as they. Tears of joy are not easily brushed away, Frank.

Frank: A pastor shares in people's lives like no other person in society, I think. It's a rare privilege and an awesome responsibility.

Jeff: Then, too, there were some of those dreams and projects that came true. Those were victorious moments. I'll not forget them. But, somehow I lost perspective. Or maybe I didn't. Maybe we do have more problems than we have answers.

Frank: Do you see any hope, Jeff?

Jeff: Oh, yes. I'm still in the church. As a matter of fact, I'm at this convention as an interested layman. I'm still very involved in the church. What about you? You're still in the ministry, I would assume you see some hope.

Frank: Yes. There's hope. I see the problems and they are real ones, but I think we shall triumph. Things even may get worse before they get better.

Jeff: Where do *you* find hope, Frank?

Frank: I find it in Jesus' promise that the gates of death would not prevail against his church. Sure, churches will die, but his church, his body, his holy people—somehow I have to believe that He will always live through us.

Jeff: I think I can find it historically in the Old Testament remnant, that small but faithful band of people who remained his.

Frank: The juniper tree, remember?

Jeff: What about it?

Frank: Well, it's usually employed as a symbol to portray men of God under duress sitting under it with their lament. But do you remember God's answer to Elijah when he had despaired? He moved him beyond the juniper tree to the place where he revealed to him that—

Jeff: [*Interrupts.*] Yes, that there were seven thousand who had not yet sold out to Baal. And not only that, he chose Elijah's successor. That's a tremendous catalogue of hope: a God who ministers to us under the juniper tree of despair; gives us a reminder of the remnant; shares with us the assurance that there will always be a successor to the prophet with substance.

Frank: The trouble with us is that we've made the juniper tree a stopping place instead of a way station along the pilgrimage in the prophetic task.

Jeff: Do you know why I'm still in the church? I read one evening in a moment of dark silence a quote from Monia Furlong. It's my fingernail-in-the-cliff. It keeps me hanging on. I've committed it to memory. "Within the struggling, sprawling, quarreling mass of the churches, within their stifling narrowness, their ignorance, their insensitivity, their stupidity, their fear of the senses and of truth, I perceive another Church, one which really is Christ at work in the world. To this Church men seem to be admitted as much by a baptism of the heart as of the body, and they know more of intellectual charity, of vulnerability, of love, of joy, of peace, than most of the rest of us. They have learned to live with few defences and so conquered the isolation which torments me. They do not judge, especially morally; their own relationships make it possible for others to grow. It does not matter what their circumstances are, what their physical and mental limitations are. They really are free men, the prisoners who have been released and who in turn can release others."[3]

Frank: That's what it's all about, Jeff. The remnant will always be. Next time I camp under the juniper tree I'll remember our time together. And I'll see it as a resting place, not the final stop in my prophetic task!

Jeff: Great! Let's get on to the convention.

NOTES

[1] Reinhold Niebuhr, *Leaves from the Notebook of a Tamed Cynic,* (Cleveland: Meridian Books, The World Publishing Company, 1929), p. 201.

[2] Ibid., pp. 97–98.

[3] Monia Furlong, *With Love to the Church,* quoted in Leslie Weatherhead, *The Christian Agnostic* (Nashville: Abingdon Press, 1965), p. 158.

I saw a fantastic sight the other day, Jack. A hippie on a motor-cycle had pulled up to a red light. A little lady in a red Volkswagen pulled up by him. She rolled down the window, said something, and then she just spat on him! As the light changed and she rolled away I saw her bumper sticker: "See you in church on Sunday."—
Laura

A Coffee-Cup Chat, or
An Early Morning Peek
at Prejudice

"I do not understand what I do; for I don't do what I would like to do, but instead I do what I hate."—Paul in *Romans 7:15*

"He who says that he is in the light, yet hates his brother, is in the darkness to this very hour. . . . He walks in it, and he does not know where he is going, because the darkness has made him blind."—John in *1 John 2:9–11*

"God treats all men alike."—Simon Peter in *Acts 10:34*

"Do not think of yourselves more highly than you should."—Paul in *Romans 12:3*

Jack: Good morning, Laura. Am I to understand that our charming instructor of history has no eight o'clock class this semester?

Laura: Oh, good morning, Jack. Some stroke of good fortune must have prevailed for once in my brief career at Peak University. No eight o'clock class. How are you this morning?

Jack: Squint-eyed and web-brained. Too early. Too early. Well, can the chaplain of said university join you in an early morning cup of coffee?

Laura: Of course. The student center's almost empty now, but about 8:30—wow! It'll be the return of the Goths!

Jack: Come now, the students aren't *that* bad!

Laura: No, of course not. I'm really kidding. By the way, I wanted to tell you how much I appreciated your chapel sermon yesterday. It was one of the keenest messages on some of the problems Jesus faced that I've ever heard. You mentioned one concern that I would like to hear you complete one day.

Jack: Oh? Which one was that?

Laura: This idea of Jesus' facing the prejudice of his day, his world. Especially religious people who were among the most prejudiced.

Jack: It's an age-old problem, prejudice. There's so much of it today I thought it might be helpful to remind us that Jesus had it too, if there's any comfort in shared misery!

Laura: But the difference is that it seems so much more pervasive today. Blacks and whites, labor and management, conservatives and liberals, North and South, the young and the old: all these have their resentments against the other.

Jack: That's what I was trying to say. Jesus lived in the same kind of world. Jew hated Samaritan, Gentile hated Jew, Roman hated everyone not Roman, slaves hated free men and free men flaunted their advantages in the faces of slaves. Every in-group has an out-group, Laura.

Laura: I know. Women were despised because of their sex, and still are in some situations. Tax collectors soaked their constituents and the people hated every available revenue man. The zealots hated Rome and Rome hated back any who preached revolution and rebellion.

Jack: Right. One of the students asked the other day if Jesus ever really had a chance. He put it this way: "How do you change persons who can't and won't focus their resentments?"

Laura: Now that's what I was going to ask you! I remember

25

getting turned on by the way Carlyle Marney once put it: "A prejudiced man is a man who cannot change his mind about his resentments. Don't get in position where your resentments cannot be changed—focus your resentments where they belong."[1] I've been intrigued by this prejudice thing for a long time. Every period of history has it. Prejudice is a part of man. Why, Jack?

Jack: I've spent hundreds of hours on that question, Laura. It seems to me that prejudice arises not out of any essential differences between people, not out of any superiority or inferiority, not out of social pressures, but simply out of the will of every person, in Paul's words, "to think more highly of himself than he ought to think."

Laura: Sort of the attempt of a person to play God, to pretend he has all the truth?

Jack: I think so. And heaven knows the church has been guilty of this throughout history.

Laura: Yes, I'm sure Galileo would testify to that fact.

Jack: What? Who?

Laura: Galileo! I was reading about him again the other day. The Church made him recant his belief that the sun was the center of the universe. The Church of his day still held a geocentric belief.

Jack: Yes, I remember. He did recant, didn't he?

Laura: Yes, but the story is that as he left the bench he whispered, "Si pur muove."

Jack: Translation?

Laura: "But it does move!" Copernicus had the same beliefs but he didn't press them as earnestly as Galileo.

Jack: That's a good example, Laura. Some of the bitterest prejudice and hatred have come from Christian people.

Laura: Brussels, October 6, 1536. Remember?

Jack: You historians, always reciting dates and places! Refresh my memory.

Laura: Tyndale, William. Crime? Translating the Scriptures into the tongue of the common man. Punishment? Strangulation and burning at the stake.

Jack: Of course, I remember. Now I have one. Champel, Switzerland, October 27, 1553.

Laura: That's easy. Michael Servetus. Crime? Irregular views of the Trinity. Accuser? John Calvin and the Geneva court. History's list is long with such events. But I think you're right, Jack.

Jack: About what?

Laura: In most situations some person or groups will set themselves up as judge. They determine what truth is with something of a superior-inferior scale of values. Everyone is then judged by that scale.

Jack: I think that's an accurate appraisal. Prejudice is man's perverted expression of the will to be God.

Laura: But there were some things you didn't get to say in your sermon yesterday. At least I felt there were.

Jack: Yes. Time lapsed before I could deliver all my thoughts. I was going to say that one of the reasons Jesus experienced so much prejudice was because of his beginnings.

Laura: I don't quite follow you.

Jack: Well, look at the way he began. There surely must have been some cautious whispers about Mary's circumstances while she was pregnant. And in a small town those back-alley whispers, those glances cast askance can prejudice a community against a child before he's born.

Laura: I see what you mean. And even after he had become a man and had begun his ministry he met the salty sneers, the raised eyebrows and the skeptical quip, "Can any good come out of Nazareth?" They were really saying that anyone who began in Nazareth just couldn't possibly have it.

Jack: And that's a part of prejudice. Provincial blindness, I call it. Those first-century cynics are still with us. There are always those who see no hope in something because no hope has ever been seen there before.

Laura: It's ironic, isn't it?

Jack: What is?

Laura: Here we are with our self-cleaning ovens, air-conditioned autos, well-tailored clothes, and push-button homes, and we haven't learned to live person with person.

Jack: Tragically true. A man's beginnings still get in our way. Sectioned-off suburbs, blue-blood country clubs, tightly restricted neighborhoods—

27

Laura: [*Interrupts.*] And all-white churches who have vowed, with God's help, of course, to stay that way. Your point is well taken, Jack. Any way you come at the problem, it's "membership" by where you started. I see what you mean. We still judge men by how they begin.

Jack: Exactly. Wrong parents, different slant of the eyes, other side of town, different color of skin, North or South of the Mason-Dixon line: the question is not who you are but where you began.

Laura: I saw something the other day that exposed this same attitude. It's really an antisemitic reflection:

> How odd
> of God
> To choose
> The Jews.

Jack: Yes. Who would have thought that God would have begun his revelation with that people.

Laura: I just had a thought. As a historian, I think history is often kinder to the men it births. History is not prejudiced, only men.

Jack: You mean kinder than we are to one another? I don't quite understand.

Laura: I mean history eventually judges a man on his achievements, not on his beginnings. Call the roll whom history has judged well. Their beginnings frequently do not match their achievements.

Jack: I think you've got something there. Go on.

Laura: Well, take Moses. Found in a basket floating on the river among the weeds, birthed in fear, bred in deceit. Who would have guessed in a thousand years that the babe loved by the Egyptian princess would become one of the great leaders of history?

Jack: Great idea! In the same line of thought, take David. A fair-faced shepherd lad left out of the first-round examination of the sons of Jesse. A boy whose only cares were his sheep and his music, a king to unite all Israel?

Laura: Or the man I did my master's thesis on: Constantine.

Who would ever guess that a man who began when his barmaid mother in Gaul slept with a Roman general—that *this* man would pass an edict in 313 that would make most of the world Christian? At least Christian in name!

Jack: What about Martin Luther? The common ordinary son of a coal miner. Who would have guessed that from such small beginnings would come such strength and influence?

Laura: And remember William Carey? A lad who dawdled during the preacher's sermon? He finally became a cobbler. How much vision can a shoemaker have? Choose any book on Protestant mission. He's there!

Jack: You're absolutely right, Laura. History *is* kinder to the men it births. It judges them on the basis of their achievements, not just on how they began. Men ought to do the same. Prejudice that takes its cue from a person's beginnings is surely the weakest kind. [*Pauses.*] But there's another side to the matter of prejudice.

Laura: I'm listening.

Jack: Well, it seems that persons tend to be prejudiced not only about a man's beginnings, but also about his position up or down from center.

Laura: You've left me there.

Jack: I remember a lecture Harold Cooke Phillips once gave in preaching class. He said that men crucify two types of people. Those who fall too far *below* the standard of the masses and those who rise too far *above* that standard.

Laura: Oh, I see. Say, some of those I mentioned earlier were too far ahead of their time. I guess that's what you meant when you said, "above the standard." Copernicus, Galileo, almost all the greats in history.

Jack: This is what I meant about Jesus, too. I think he was so far ahead, "above" his time that he aroused fierce prejudice and resentment in the people.

Laura: Anyone who is different really is subject to prejudice. And being above or below the masses is clearly a way of being different.

Jack: And it's no coincidence that both kinds were on Calvary, Laura. There were two thieves—those below the norm; and there was Jesus—the one above the norm.

Laura: I had never seen it that way before. That's a thought to chew on!

Jack: I remember a quote from Eric Hoffer that I used in a sermon once: "Whence come these unreasonable hatreds, and their unifying effect? They are an expression of a desperate effort to suppress an awareness of our inadequacy, worthlessness, guilt, and other shortcomings of the self. Self-contempt is here transmuted into hatred of others— and there is a most determined and persistent effort to mask this switch."[2]

Laura: That's great insight. People hate those above them because they are reminded of their own inadequacies! They hate those below them because they fear these qualities are in them, too. Surely, this is the stuff of which crucifixions are made!

Jack: Right. And we can certainly understand why Jesus found so much resentment. He spoke no current shibboleths, no hackneyed clichés that marked the religious language of the day.

Laura: And he refused to guarantee anything apart from a cross carried daily. That kind of message, like wrong beginnings, induces resentment and prejudice in the majority and love only in the "open" majority.

Jack: Prejudice is not restricted just to race, color, or creed, though. It raises its head rather against the *differentness* of race, color, or creed.

Laura: I saw a fantastic sight the other day, Jack. A hippie on a motorcycle had pulled up to a red light. A little lady in a red Volkswagen pulled up by him. She rolled down the window, said something, and then she just spat on him! As the light changed and she rolled away, I saw her bumper sticker: "See you in church on Sunday." She's probably a very pious Christian on Sundays! Anyway, it shows that differentness you spoke about.

Jack: It's always a marvel to me how he who was so different has been made so conformist. That little woman didn't even know that boy. He was different, therefore evil, and therefore deserved to be spit on.

Laura: Different! Is that the reason the Christian church in

America is still one of the most segregated, fearful, up-tight institutions around?

Jack: Ouch! I feel my chaplain's status underfoot!

Laura: Nothing personal, Jack. But the gospel as I understand it is the most beautiful thing in man's total history. Yet it comes through like so much watered-down wine to an alcoholic thirst.

Jack: I know as white, Anglo-Saxon, middle-class Protestants, we seem to have made the same mistake that Israel made in her history.

Laura: Which was?

Jack: Feeling that God's election is due to our goodness instead of his grace. And it follows that if I feel I have been chosen for my goodness, I must have an extra special "something." Therefore, those who don't appear to be chosen must not have this something. And I come through this whole business of grace with a feeling of superiority.

Laura: Well, that helps me to understand, but my feeling is the same. The church has allowed to exist a system of life and thought that has fostered prejudice of all kinds. Class, race, heritage—

Jack: [*Interrupts.*] And don't forget theological witch-hunts! Some of our denomination conventions always threaten to put new meat on the skeleton of Calvin and his court waiting in the wings!

Laura: I guess Dostoyevsky was right. He once described man as the "ungrateful biped." He could have said just as easily the "prejudiced biped."

Jack: Yes. And when you boil it all down I guess that Jesus and his methods, his love, his faith stood far above that of average man. They didn't understand. Men fear what they do not understand, and they eliminate what they fear. You were right a moment ago, Laura. This is the stuff, the structure, the shape, the design of crosses that are made by hands that fear.

Laura: That cross—his cross, Jack—it's really a way of taking everything we're prejudiced against: beginnings, projected hatreds, one different by being above or below the average, and getting them off our backs.

Jack: Right. And in that sense the answer is yes to the old Negro spiritual, "Were You There When They Crucified My Lord?"

Laura: How that speaks to history! Talaat Pasha did not exterminate millions of Armenians alone. Hitler alone did not roast millions of Jews. And the Jews and Romans did not single-handedly nail God to a tree, either!

Jack: No! He became not just a sad, pitiful figure of the first century, but a scapegoat for all our prejudices and sins. Think of it. A Man whose beginnings, birth, message, visions and dreams were different. . . .

Laura: [*Interrupts.*] Too tall for his times—and ours. Do you remember what Aldous Huxley says in *Eyeless in Gaza?* ". . . If you don't treat men as men they don't behave as men"?[3]

Jack: Yes. But God goes Huxley one better. He treats us like men even when we don't behave like men. And that's our redemption, Laura. Redemption is all about one Man who took all that prejudice had to dish out and loved right through it.

Laura: And he still does, Jack. Somehow, he still does. When we let him, that is.

NOTES

[1] Carlyle Marney, *Beggars in Velvet* (Nashville: Abingdon Press, 1960) p. 62.

[2] Eric Hoffer, *The True Believer*, quoted by Levon G. King, "The Enemy Within," *Pulpit Digest* (January 1970), p. 24.

[3] Aldous Huxley, *Eyeless in Gaza*, quoted in Kyle Haseldon, *The Racial Problem in Christian Perspective* (Evanston: Harper Torchbooks, 1959), p. 137.

Peter, let's look at it this way. There comes a time when love doesn't calculate. It doesn't ask, "How little can I give and still look decent and respectable?" And when we see a love that refuses to count the cost, it looks strangely excessive to us. True love has a way of embarrassing the world. It outrages respectability.—John

"Psst! John!
About That Woman..."

Jesus was in the house of Simon the leper, in Bethany; while he was eating, a woman came in with an alabaster jar full of a very expensive perfume, made of pure nard. She broke the jar and poured the perfume on Jesus' head. Some of the people there became angry, and said to each other, "What was the use of wasting the perfume? It could have been sold for more than three hundred dollars, and the money given to the poor!" And they criticized her harshly. But Jesus said: "Leave her alone! Why are you bothering her? She has done a fine and beautiful thing for me. You will always have poor people with you, and any time you want to you can help them. But I shall not be with you always. She did what she could: she poured perfume on my body to prepare it for burial ahead of time. Now, remember this! Wherever the gospel is preached, all over the world, what she has done will be told in memory of her."

Then Judas Iscariot, one of the twelve disciples, went off to the chief priests in order to hand Jesus over to them. They were greatly pleased to hear what he had to say, and promised to give him money. So Judas started looking for a good chance to betray Jesus.—*Mark 14:3–11*

Peter: [*Whispers.*] Psst! John. Back here.

John: What's the matter, Peter?

Peter: Let the others go on ahead. I want to ask you something.

John: Well, make it quick, I had planned to talk with Jesus about something.

Peter: No, hang back with me. We'll be in Bethany in a few minutes. Let the others go on ahead. I've got a question about what happened in Jerusalem today, at Simon's house. John, about that woman—

John: [*Interrupts.*] Oh, you mean at Simon the leper's. The woman who poured perfume on Jesus? That was a beautiful act!

Peter: That's what I want to ask you about. Jesus interpreted it as beautiful, too. As for me, it was a pathetic waste!

John: How can you say that, Peter? Where's your sense of the profound, the beautiful? For instance, just look at this time of the day. There's nothing more thrilling than to see the sun slipping weary-like behind earth's edge as if, having spent itself in fierce heat, it willingly becomes a giant ember slowly cooling into quiet blackness. And the stars just beginning to wink—

Peter: [*Interrupts.*] All right, John! I didn't mean to get you started. But your ability to see into things, that's why I wanted to talk with you. I've often told the others that while you're a fisherman like the rest of us—

John: [*Interrupts.*] And a good one!

Peter: Under that rough exterior you have the soul of a poet.

John: [*Humorously.*] Thank you, my good man.

Peter: No, I'm serious, John. You may not think I've noticed, and it's not easy for me to say. But . . . well, you have something special. I sometimes feel that Jesus loves you a little more.

John: Come, now, Peter!

Peter: No, there's a closeness there. Your souls speak a common language.

John: But he takes you and James with him on our special assignments, too.

Peter: Yes, but I always feel James and I need it. But you—

Well, James and I are disciples, but you're a companion to Jesus. There's a difference. But I didn't call you back here just to say that. I want you to explain to me why Jesus got so excited and thrilled when that woman broke the jar of perfume and anointed him.

John: It was an expression of her love, Peter. That's all. You remember, of course, that Jesus had forgiven her some time ago. She simply expressed her gratitude.

Peter: [*Interrupts.*] But with pure nard, John? That stuff was expensive. Three hundred denarii worth of fragrance, and for what? The way we have to work, that's about a year's wages. Philip said it would have taken that much to have fed the five thousand. That's not extravagance, that's insanity!

John: But he accepted the act and praised the woman for what she had done.

Peter: That's what really disturbs me. If she wants to waste three hundred denarii I guess that's her business, but for Jesus to condone such a flagrant waste—!

John: Three years and nothing done!

Peter: What are you talking about?

John: You, Peter. You've spent three years in intimate fellowship with Jesus and you still don't understand. What he did at Simon's didn't surprise me. That's the way he's always been with gifts.

Peter: I don't understand.

John: He always looks behind the gift to the motive. You know that. He seldom takes anything at its face value. He always gets behind the gift to the reason it was given—or withheld, whichever the case may be.

Peter: Oh, yeah, I remember. The young ruler who wanted to become one of us. And that widow who dropped in two copper coins. He became very excited about her gift.

John: What I'm saying is that with Jesus it's not how much something costs. It's how much it costs *the person*. The value of the gift is relative. For one who could have afforded it, the nard wouldn't have been such an impressive gift. For the woman, it was everything.

Peter: What you're saying is that a thimbleful of second-rate perfume wouldn't have said what the woman felt, right?

John: Right!

Peter: But maybe she could have told him it was the thought—

John: [*Interrupts.*] None of that "it's the thought that counts" business. The woman didn't love that way. After all, he forgave her sins. He didn't just walk up to her and say, "I'll be thinking about you."

Peter: Confound it, John. You're just like he is. You never leave me a cliché to stand on. Since we have been with him I don't have a saying or a cliché intact!

John: You're better off without them. They oversimplify when they're right but most of the time they're empty of truth. Anyway, what I was saying. That woman's *valeriana jatamansi*—

Peter: [*Interrupts.*] There you go with those high-sounding words again.

John: [*Interrupts.*] Well, that's what it was. That was the widow's mite in liquid form! It is the most precious thing she had.

Peter: Well, I'll say one thing. I'm glad she's not my wife. Three hundred denarii of perfume on a man's head! Why, she'd blow the grocery money on a jar of perfume, souse the head of her current hero, and come home with an empty grocery basket and a hollow jar!

John: I'm not sure you've really seen it yet.

Peter: I'm not either. I'm not sure I want to see it.

John: Peter, let's look at it this way. There comes a time when love doesn't calculate. It doesn't ask, "How little can I give and still look decent and respectable?" And when we see a love that refuses to count the cost, it looks strangely excessive to us. True love has a way of embarrassing the world. It outrages respectability.

Peter: It outraged mine!

John: There comes a time, Peter, when you can't trade beauty for a bargain. Now Judas would gladly have traded that jar of graciousness for a basket of groceries. But then, that's Judas.

Peter: And a lot of us if the truth were known. Most of us were quiet when she emptied the jar on his head and we would not have dared to say anything when the Master praised

36

her. But down deep, I knew what we were all feeling. Except maybe for you.

John: I knew how you were feeling, too. I could see it in your face. It was the same expression you had when Jesus let Mary sit at his feet and Martha had to do all the cooking. Your face is the mirror of your soul, Peter.

Peter: But, now, think about it, John. Let men who have no home, little food, and only the clothes on their backs—you let that kind of men watch three hundred denarii get poured on a man's head, and you've got anxiety.

John: You also have men who know the cost of everything but the value of nothing.

Peter: Now what does that mean?

John: Cost is what it takes to get something. Value is what makes you want it. Most of us have this backwards! We become so threatened with pouring out a part of ourselves—

Peter: [*Interrupts.*] You're right! That's a great thought. I'm beginning to see your point now. Say, no wonder we weren't able to understand that woman's selfless gift. Do you realize that it wasn't but just a few days back that we were all at each other's throats about who was the greatest and who was going to be on which side of Jesus? We're still so full of ourselves we can't appreciate a selfless act when we see one. This is what you've been saying. Isn't it?

John: Bravo! Finally! I never know what's going to get the point across to you, Peter. You're as unpredictable as the Sea of Galilee out of which your discipleship was spawned. But now that you've got the point, I wonder if we've really believed that it makes a difference.

Peter: That what does?

John: That we can see beauty for beauty's sake. Truth, love, gifts, for their own sakes.

Peter: You think it does matter?

John: I know it does. If we can't see, hear, and respond to beauty, innocence, tenderness, and expressions of love's extravagance, how can we see the beauty in the Master? Is an insensitive soul suddenly going to develop tender sensitivities when he comes to Jesus?

Peter: I remember something he said about that. If I can quote it: "Your eyes are like a lamp for the body: when your eyes are clear your whole body is full of light; but when your eyes are bad your whole body will be in darkness." You remember that?

John: Yes. Our lives, like our eyes, must always be open to him. This is why he is fond of children. This is also the same reason he liked the woman's gift today.

Peter: And to think I tried to hold back the youngsters when they came to him. "Not now," I said to them. "He's busy teaching the adults."

John: The way he held out his hands to them! He was saying these were his kind of people. The child kind, the innocent kind, the open kind.

Peter: [*Reflectively.*] John, do you think that's why he chose us and not the Pharisees! Heaven knows they're smarter than we are.

John: Yes. But they aren't as open. I asked him about that one night when the rest of you were sleeping. He never answered directly, but he said that only a fool would try to pour wine into a skin already full.

Peter: We're more teachable?

John: That's what he was saying. The Pharisees will never understand what that woman did. But we . . . well, we'll eventually get the point. It'll take time, but we'll get it.

Peter: I have another question about what happened with the woman and her perfume. What do you think he meant by, "You'll always have the poor with you"?

John: Well, we know how much he cares for the poor. He wasn't saying we ought to be unconcerned for them. It's all tied up with what he said about his not being here always.

Peter: That bothered me, too. I wonder what he meant? In fact, that's the third or fourth time he's made a statement like that in the last several weeks.

John: I think he must be saying that there are some things we can do only once, and to miss the moment is to forfeit the opportunity. "Be sure you do the things today that can't wait until tomorrow. There are some things that lose their value by tomorrow." Eleazar the rabbi used to say that a lot.

Peter: But what did he mean by "not being with us"? And

didn't I hear him say something about her anointing him for burial? What was he talking about?

John: You remember just before we came into Jerusalem this last time? He said something one day about being delivered into the hands of the chief priests, the elders, and others. He talked about death then, too.

Peter: You don't think he would leave us now, do you? After three years? We're just beginning to catch on. If he were just to up and leave—

John: [*Interrupts.*] I have a haunting, hollow feeling, Peter. When he rode into Jerusalem on the ass the other day the people were screaming, "Hosanna, Hosanna," and they were spreading palms and garments in front of him. But their talk—

Peter: [*Interrupts.*] I know. I heard it, too. They were referring to him as Messiah all right. But it wasn't the kind of messiah I had understood.

John: I know. I think the people expect a military messiah like King David.

Peter: Well, if what we discussed at Caesarea Philippi is true, he's not *that* kind of messiah.

John: Exactly, and that's what bothers me. The people are expecting him to be one kind of messiah and the religious leaders are responding to him as that kind. They're threatened by his popularity. They fear what they think him to be.

Peter: But the Romans probably see him as a political messiah. Man! He could get it from all sides. And we with him! But wait a minute. What has this to do with the woman's anointing him?

John: You were questioning his remarks about not being with us and her preparing him for burial, remember? Heavens! What a mind!

Peter: All right, I'm with you again.

John: By the way, have you seen the leaders huddled together this past week? Get that many legalists together in one place and they're up to no good!

Peter: You mean they're trying to have him—

John: Killed! I've been adding it all up for days, Peter. And when he said what he did to the woman about preparation for burial, I knew. That's why I was on my way up to talk to him when you called me back here.

Peter: You know, I was just thinking. If we go back to Jerusalem tomorrow and something happens to him, this act of "beauty," as you call it, could be one of the last expressions of real love shown him, couldn't it?

John: It could! And as such it will always be remembered as the last act of goodness before—

Peter: [*Interrupts.*] I would rather not talk about it any more! I don't like what we're thinking. But I will confess I've been reflecting along the same lines as you. And I know James and Matthew have. I talked to them last night after the meal. None of us will talk about it. There's something so final about putting your fears into words. Like they either have to come true or leave you.

John: Some of the others are coming to the same conclusions, too. Look at them up ahead. None of them talking together. Each lost in his own thoughts. They feel it too.

Peter: You know, looking back, John, I don't see how I could have gotten so angry today. When the woman did that, I mean.

John: Well, you're certainly not known for your self-control, Peter. But speaking of anger, did you see Judas? I've never seen him so mad.

Peter: Yes. He left in a huff, didn't he? He threw down the money pouch we keep for the poor as if to say, "That's the last straw," and stalked out.

John: Just between us, I wonder about Judas. I've noticed that the last several days he leaves the rest of us as soon as we get into Jerusalem. I wonder where he goes?

Peter: Well, I've suspected for a long time that he's had his hand in the money pouch for the poor. That's probably why he wanted to sell the perfume, so he could get his hands on the money!

John: That's possible. But, Peter, I've had another thought. I've hesitated to mention it. Don't you dare speak a word of this to anyone. But . . . well . . . [*Whispers.*] do you think it possible that Judas is selling out?

Peter: John! Judas? Sell—

John: Shhh! I told you. Quiet!

Peter: I think he may be a thief, but to sell us out? I had not thought of it. But then there's a lot I miss, it seems.

John: As we've talked I've kinda put it all together. Jesus has been talking in recent weeks about his death. He seems preoccupied with it. The entry into Jerusalem showed a lot of wrong expectations. The sharp questions this week from the religious leaders—

Peter: [*Interrupts.*] Jesus' rampage in the Temple, his teachings that clearly upset everyone, Judas' absence from us and his anger at the anointing—

John: And Jesus' reference to his burial and his prediction that this act would be remembered. I see a pattern that frightens me.

Peter: Wait a minute, John. If what we're talking about comes to pass, if he's . . . killed, if he gives his life for his cause, then that could explain his sensitivity to gifts. That's it. That's why he responded so.

John: Caesarea Philippi all over again! Beautiful, Peter. If he's ready to give his life, then naturally the whole concept of giving is on the edge of his mind. Sure! That must have something to do with it.

Peter: And it would explain that remark about burial.

John: Right. One so near giving an ultimate gift would naturally realize the value of such a gift as she gave!

Peter: That woman, John. There was more in that act than love's gracious gift. I mean it *was* that, but she has helped us to fit together some missing pieces. I hope we're wrong but I have a strong feeling we're dead right.

John: I think we are. I pray we're not. Well, I see that Bethany is just around the bend. Lazarus, Mary, and Martha will want to know about the day's events so there'll be no chance for further talk. I want to speak to Jesus before we get there. I'll see you later.

Peter: All right. And, John, thanks for your insight. Peace.

John: Peace.

He's a false prophet, Nicodemus. Miracles, wise sayings, parables—all fake. And if you really need proof look at that ragtag bunch of disciples. No sane man would surround himself with that kind. Why, look at Andrew and Bartholomew. We've known those boys for years and two more shy lads you couldn't find. And that big, bungling fisherman, Simon. What a laugh! You can tell a leader by the kind of followers he inspires. That group gives him away. He's a fake!—Ezra

---

"He's Turned the Tables"

When the Pharisees gathered together, Jesus asked them: "What do you think about the Messiah? Whose descendant is he?" "He is David's descendant," they answered. "Why, then," Jesus asked, "did the Spirit inspire David to call him 'Lord'? For David said,
>   'The Lord said to my Lord:
>   Sit here at my right side,
>   Until I put your enemies under your feet.'

If, then, David called him 'Lord,' how can the Messiah be David's descendant?" No one was able to answer Jesus a single word, and from that day on no one dared ask him any more questions.—*Matthew 22:41-46*

This was one of the most frustrating weeks on record for the religious leaders of Israel. The young prophet from Nazareth has been confronted daily by the sharpest minds and the keenest wits among the leaders. They have done their best to discredit the man Jesus before the people. But their failure has been his opportunity.

It all started several days ago when Jesus was teaching on

the temple steps. The chief priests and elders conspired to sabotage his teachings by asking him who gave him the authority to teach, preach, perform miracles and, in general, to sway the people with his power.

His answer to them was a question: "Was John's baptism from heaven or from men?" Knowing that the answer "from heaven" would bring the question, "Then why didn't you believe him," and that the answer "from men" would discredit them before the people, the leaders became "expediently ignorant." They answered, "We don't know."

The next "trick" question was devised by the disciples of the Pharisees and the Roman-sponsored Herodians. They pitted their wits against Jesus, asking him whether it was lawful to pay taxes to Caesar. His answer was astonishingly simple. "Give God his due, and give Caesar what belongs to him."

The Sadducees, no doubt pleased at their rival's failures, decided to try their hands at tripping Jesus. They asked Jesus about the resurrection—a strange turn of events since they didn't believe in the resurrection. Under Jewish law, when a man died, his brother was obligated to marry his widow and have children by her. The children would be considered the deceased man's rightful and legal offspring. The Sadducees structured a problem question in which seven brothers in succession were married to a woman, and they all died childless. Their question was, "Whose wife will she be in the resurrection?"

Jesus set them back on their heels by telling them that they knew neither the Scriptures nor the power of God. They had asked a trivial, unimportant question. "God is a God of the living, not of the dead." And the clear implications of Jesus' reply was that a living God deals with living issues.

The Pharisees came back to pose the fourth and last question to Jesus. They asked him what the great commandment was in the law. He told them to love God with all they had, and to love their neighbor as they loved themselves.

So, at least four times this week the leaders of the Jewish people have tried to embarrass, trip up, and generally discredit the Nazarene. But in every attempt they have failed.

Now it is Jesus' turn. He approaches the small group of

leaders standing on one of the temple porches. Jesus speaks: "Great leaders of Israel, I have a question for you."

"Yes, Rabbi, what is it you want to ask us?"

"What do you think of the Messiah? Whose son is he?"

The Pharisees put their collective heads together and respond to this ridiculously simple question. Every schoolboy knows the answer. The title of the Messiah is "Son of David." They give Jesus their answer, certain that he'll have no argument with that. But he does!

"Then if the Messiah is David's son, why does David, in Psalm 110, call the Messiah his Lord and not his son? Can a person be a man's son and Lord at the same time?"

Oh, no! He's done it again. He's bettered the Pharisees at their own game, and with a question out of their own Scriptures, too! None of us will ever know the consternation and frustration embodied in that one short Scriptural comment: "And no one was able to answer him a word. . . ."

As the Pharisees begin to drift away from the scene of their embarrassment, we notice two men standing on the edge of the crowd. They have been listening closely to all that has been said. They are distinguished members of the Sanhedrin, the supreme Jewish court. One is named Nicodemus, a man regarded with some suspicion by his colleagues, because it is rumored that he and the Nazarene have been having some private talks during the midnight hours for several weeks running. Nicodemus' colleague is a man named Ezra, a well-known, highly respected member of the Sanhedrin. They push through the crowd until they find one of the few quiet corners in the temple. You and I are able to follow them and lean back casually, half-hidden, on one of the columns of the temple porch. They are unaware anyone is near. We can hear them talking as Ezra speaks.

Ezra: But I tell you, Nicodemus, that was a most unorthodox interpretation of the Scriptures. I've read Psalm 110 hundreds of times. I've always accepted it as a Messianic text of Israel. But look what that Nazarene did to it. Why, he took it apart. What was he really saying, anyway, Nicodemus?

Nicodemus: Well, Ezra, it's very simple, really. Jesus pointed out that David, in his psalm, called the Messiah his Lord. Now we have always thought of the Messiah as David's son. But it's clear that a person can't be a man's son and his Lord at the same time.

Ezra: Yes, yes. I understand that. But why did he give this passage a new interpretation?

Nicodemus: Because I think Jesus is saying that it's not enough to think of the Messiah in terms of an earthly conquest. He's saying, I think, that the Messiah is more than a kingly conqueror.

Ezra: But we've always thought of it that way, Nicodemus. After all, David marks the high point in our history: one ruler, one kingdom, one God. We've always looked for the return of that kind of king with his kingdom. What's wrong with it? We've always believed it.

Nicodemus: Nothing's really wrong with it, Ezra. Only it's inadequate. It's good, maybe, but not the best. Jesus has talked to me about another kingdom—the kingdom of God, not David. This is a beautiful idea, a kingdom, a rule, a reign of God in the hearts and lives of men. It frees their hearts and—

Ezra: Fine, fine! But we need our hands and backs free, too, Nicodemus. This Roman rule is cutting our nation—and our religion—to pieces.

Nicodemus: But if a man has God's reign in his life he can endure even Roman rule, Ezra. What Jesus is talking about is something that helps you live with, through, maybe even *above* your circumstances. He's talked to me in terms of trust, belief.

Ezra: Humph! A member of the Sanhedrin who acts like trust and belief are new ideas! I'm ashamed of you, Nicodemus.

Nicodemus: But it's radically different from ours, Ezra. It's not a belief in our history, or our heritage, or our law. It's belief in a person. Now to most of us Jews that's a new idea, Ezra. That's something that can get a man spiritually excited, even—

Ezra: Are you saying you *believe* this, Nicodemus? Is this radical prophet getting to you? Are you letting yourself get involved with what he's teaching?

Nicodemus: No! Oh, I don't know, Ezra. I didn't believe it at first. Those first few nights I went to talk to him I felt were just intellectual exercises. I didn't take him too seriously. I was a curiosity seeker. But then . . . well, Jesus is not the kind of man you can hold at arm's length, Ezra. There's no middle ground with him.

Ezra: That's easy to see. The city is divided into two camps, those for him and those against him. No middle ground, indeed. I wish there were, for our sakes.

Nicodemus: No. You either have to push him away or bring him close. But *you* have to do it, Ezra. I got the feeling as I talked to him in those night hours that what I decided about him was on my shoulders; he was just there. But *I* had to decide. And no matter what we talked about there was that feeling that in some way a decision was hanging in the balance. Does that make sense?

Ezra: It does to me. You're losing your mind over a third-rate prophet!

Nicodemus: No! Listen, Ezra. I'm not sure how much I believe about what he says. There are many questions unanswered. But I trust him, Ezra, and somehow that's what seems most important. It's that personal relationship that really matters. Ah, but enough of this. How do *you* answer his question, Ezra? You know, he turned the tables on us. We've been asking him questions. But now he's asked us one.

Ezra: When? What are you talking about? I've never seen a sane man babble so—

Nicodemus: Have you forgotten so soon? "What do you think of the Messiah?" That's the question. No! Let's go one better. Suppose *he* is the Messiah; suppose those who spread the palms before him last week were right? Suppose he is the anointed one. What do *you* think of him?

Ezra: Well, in the first place he's *not* the anointed one. Read the Scriptures. Does he look like the kind of Messiah we find there? No. I can't go along. He's a false prophet, Nicodemus. Miracles, wise sayings, parables—all fake. And if you really need proof look at that ragtag bunch of disciples.

Nicodemus: They are good men, Ezra. Oh, I know some of our colleagues think they lack the proper credentials, but—

Ezra: No sane man would surround himself with *that* kind. Why, look at Andrew and Bartholomew. We've known those boys for years and two more shy lads you couldn't find. And that big, bungling fisherman, Simon. What a laugh! You can tell a leader by the kind of followers he inspires. *That* group gives him away. He's a fake.

Nicodemus: But some of them are changing, Ezra.

Ezra: Nonsense. When he dies they'll run like a pack of frightened dogs! But besides that, explain to me how God's Messiah can undo all God's laws? Why, this man has disregarded most of the law and prophets. And he has consistently worked on the Sabbath: healing, preaching, teaching his strange ideas. How do you explain this?

Nicodemus: Maybe we've never really understood the law, Ezra. He's talked to me about fulfilling the law and the prophets. And when you get to the motives and intentions behind the laws that makes sense. But what made most sense was the way he talked about eternal life.

Ezra: Eternal life?

Nicodemus: Yes, yes. Let me tell you about it. It has to do with the kind of life a man lives.

Ezra: It sounds like living a long time. Eternal life—

Nicodemus: No. Not just living a long time. Living a quality life. A life above board, one with meaning and purpose. It has something to say about how you and I get along as men—brothers, Jesus would say.

Ezra: Our law covers all that.

Nicodemus: Yes, but it's a step above law, yet, it believes in law, too. It's like obeying law not because you *have* to— that's you and me, Ezra—but because you *want* to. That makes a difference, Ezra, it really does.

Ezra: You do believe this, Nicodemus. I can see it in your eyes. You're committed to this Nazarene. Can it be?

Nicodemus: Maybe more than I've admitted, Ezra.

Ezra: No, Nicodemus. There's too much at stake. You're a

member of the Sanhedrin. You have your standing in the community, your scholarship, your good name. If you follow this Nazarene you'll throw it away. Don't do it, Nicodemus, there's too much to risk.

Nicodemus: Right! There's always risk in our lives, Ezra. And if you ask me, that's one thing that's wrong with Judaism now. All rules, no risks. We've taken all the adventure out of faith.

Ezra: Old Rabbi Elihu used to teach that venture in faith causes anxiety.

Nicodemus: Yes, but he also taught that *not* to venture was to lose one's selfhood. Jesus has awakened me, Ezra. I'm willing to say yes to life again. I'm willing to put all that I am on the belief that I can trust this man to my grave—maybe even beyond. Can't you feel that when you're near him?

Ezra: No. I think my good friend Zacharias is right about this fellow.

Nicodemus: What does he say?

Ezra: He says it's all very simple. The fellow's a crackpot. Now Zacharias has a good point about the way to live life. He says watch your talk, abide by the rules, stay in the middle of the road. Don't get involved in these deep questions. Faith, he says, is made of right thoughts. A good attitude is hard to beat. So, with Jesus, there's just no question about it. If he doesn't abide by the rules he can't be God's man. That's all there is to it. You just—

Nicodemus: Stop it! That's not all there is to it, Ezra. What about his answers that stumped all of us? They were right out of our own Scriptures. We didn't see them. We didn't because they went against our traditions. We've put our traditions on the same level with the Scriptures! We've been reading the Scriptures with our own bias.

Ezra: Of course we do, Nicodemus. Each of us brings his own interpretation. Hillel, Shammai, and other schools of thought as well—we all bring our personal heritage to the Scriptures.

Nicodemus: But Jesus has come along and breathed new life into them. The kind of religion you and Zacharias describe is what's wrong with Judaism. You've made it into a cradle where men stay spiritual babes. That's wrong, Ezra. Maybe that's the trouble. Jesus has faith that grows and stretches us all. You can't get by just by giving him pat answers. And you saw what he did to our pat questions.

Ezra: I'll swear by father Abraham you've lost yourself over this man, Nicodemus.

Nicodemus: No, Ezra: I've found something in him. It was that question he asked a few minutes ago. It was when he turned the tables on us, when he put a question before *us* for a change. That's when it happened to me, Ezra. I can't get away from it. It keeps washing up on the shore of my mind. "What do *you* think of the Christ?"

Ezra: Well, if he were here I would tell you. But Jesus is not the one!

Nicodemus: That's what he's saying, Ezra. He's telling us that he's the Christ. And he's asking you and me where we stand with him. That's the way with him. He just demands to know how you stand with him. You've got to answer that question, too, Ezra. Every man has to answer it sometime, somehow, somewhere.

Ezra: Why? Why? What's so urgent about it?

Nicodemus: Because it's a question about how life gets lived. It's a question about what's most important in life and what's not. It's the question of who's going to be Lord of life. It's a question of whether we're going to let life's little battles defeat us or let him defeat them. It's a question of mastering our hostilities or letting them master us.

Ezra: The law! The law! The law! It covers all that. It tells us what to do in almost every situation, Nicodemus. If you can read, it's in clear terms right before you.

Nicodemus: Ah! That's what shakes me, Nicodemus, an old Jew. This man doesn't come *up* with an answer like the law. He comes *as* the answer himself. Maybe that's the difference between men and God. Men come with answers. God comes as the answer—himself.

Ezra: But this thing of commitment. It bothers me, Nicodemus. You'll lose your standing, everything—

Nicodemus: But it's worth it, Ezra. What good is all the standing and the prestige in the world if life is off-center? And a lot of our religion is off-center, Ezra. But this man doesn't deal with life's periphery. He gets to the heart of things—of men.

Ezra: It appears he's gotten to you well enough.

Nicodemus: That's what commitment is all about—having this man, his values, his principles, his ideals, his eternal, abundant life at the center of your life, at the hub of who you are. I believe that, Ezra, I believe that. I really do.

You and I, standing half-hidden behind that porch column, find that tears are finding their way down our cheeks. For we've been on a search, too. And now there's something that rings eternally true about the belief in Nicodemus' voice.

We take off at a trot to find the Nazarene. We push through the crowds, jostle the merchants, bump against the money-changers, brush quickly past the priests. We find that band of followers and we elbow our way to the center of them. There he is! Our eyes meet and he asks that same question of us: "What do you think of the Christ?"

And we reach out hesitatingly, haltingly—but we *do* reach out. And we grasp his waiting hand, and the confession is wrenched from us: "My Lord . . . and . . . my God!"

But I don't care any more about all your high and mighty ideas, your searching spirit, your intellectual integrity. I'm sick and tired of seeing the man I love with rotting flesh and running sores. If you take my advice, you'll curse God and die, you'll blaspheme him and let him take out his vengeance on you in death. Death can't be worse than this. Curse God and be done with this suffering madness. Life has whipped you, Job, admit it!—Zipporah

Curse God and Die!

Again there was a day when the sons of God came to present themselves before the Lord, and Satan also came among them to present himself before the Lord. And the Lord said to Satan, "Whence have you come?" Satan answered the Lord, "From going to and fro on the earth, and from walking up and down on it." And the Lord said to Satan, "Have you considered my servant Job, that there is none like him on the earth, a blameless and upright man, who fears God and turns away from evil? He still holds fast his integrity, although you moved me against him, to destroy him without cause." Then Satan answered the Lord, "Skin for skin! All that a man has he will give for his life. But put forth thy hand now, and touch his bone and his flesh, and he will curse thee to thy face." And the Lord said to Satan, "Behold, he is in your power; only spare his life."

So Satan went forth from the presence of the Lord, and afflicted Job with loathsome sores from the sole of his foot to the crown of his head. And he took a potsherd with which to scrape himself, and sat among the ashes.

Then his wife said to him, "Do you still hold fast your integrity? Curse God, and die." But he said to her, "You speak as one of the foolish women would speak. Shall we receive good at the hand of God, and shall we not receive evil?" In all this Job did not sin with his lips.—*Job 2:1–10, RSV*

The time is about 700 B.C. The place at the edge of the desert on the land owned by a wealthy farmer and merchant named Job. He is a man who is respected by his friends and neighbors, a man of means and a person of considerable wisdom.

As we draw near to his great tent we find a startling, shocking scene. The man, Job, sits in front of his tent, half-nude in an ash heap. His head is bowed, and bald, freshly shaven. His shoulders are stooped as if he were carrying the weight of the world. His body is covered with running sores, and he scratches his burning, stinging limbs with a piece of broken pottery.

The scene is quiet, almost desolate. The household dogs, aware that something is amiss, whine anxiously and sniff hopefully around the edge of the tent in search of a crust of bread or a scrap of meat. The dry desert breeze whips the crystal white sand into little funnels and dances them from dune to dune.

The scene spells despair.

There is a rustling within the tent. The front flaps part and a woman emerges. She sits down forlornly beside her husband. She speaks to him.

Zipporah: I can't believe it, Job. It's as if the whole world has fallen in on us. The list of catastrophes reads like a nightmare, a horrible dream. First the Sabeans kill our servants and take all our work animals.

Job: Then that freakish lightning storm destroys all our sheep. Those fiendish Chaldeans raid the camel farm and all we are left with is our children, our beloved children. Then comes the news that *they* have been killed by that dastardly windstorm that tumbled their house in on them.

Zipporah: Can you believe it, Job? All our offspring wiped out by a puff of wind! Our army of servants reduced to a quartet. And now—now you sit here with those running sores from the soles of your feet to the crown of your head. Oh, Job, what are we to do?

Job: Do, Zipporah, do? About past history? Nothing. No! Maybe there are at least two alternatives. We can endure and we can interpret. But that's about all we can do about what has happened to us. My misery and pain are increasing. I can only hope to outlast these dreadful sores, these running craters of suffering. No, there's very little we can do.

Zipporah: [*Quietly.*] Job, there is something we can do. I've been thinking about it in the tent. I thought about it all night. It seems that the world is out to crush us. We can let it, Job. We can give it what it wants.

Job: Give up, Zipporah?

Zipporah: Yes. I'm serious. Look at it this way. We're old now. Everything we've poured our lives into is gone. It's too late to start over and we might as well call it quits.

Job: Call it quits, now, in the midst of the drama before we know how it's to end, Zipporah? Have you no sense of the dramatic? Ring down the curtain in the middle of the play? No!

Zipporah: Why, Job. Give me one good reason. Just one.

Job: What message then would my destroyed farms, my dead children and a body full of sores—and, oh, yes, a wife who has given up her dutiful encouragement—what message of hope does that leave history?

Zipporah: History? Does your suffering have to leave a "message" for anyone, anytime, in history? That's presumption, Job—that your back full of sores, your destroyed barns and your children's grave markers have something to say to history.

Job: I believe that!

Zipporah: Ha! You not only have a capacity for patient endurance, but for an endless measure of idiocy—in the form of pride.

Job: Pride! Pride! No, Zipporah. Hope. There is meaning in this suffering. Not so much a specific purpose, but meaning. Not that God is trying to say something to me in all this—God is not so impoverished in his communication that he can't—and doesn't—speak more directly. But there is meaning in suffering. That's where we're different. I'm willing to search for that meaning. You are not.

Zipporah: You'll die in that blind search!

Job: Maybe. But I'll die reaching for courage, not crushing it against the wall of hopelessness.

Zipporah: But I'm trying to help you, Job. I want you out of your pain.

Job: But the greatest pain does not come from these sores, or from ravaged farms or even from my children crushed under falling timber. The worst pain is not knowing *why* I suffer. If I can find the why I can endure the what and the how for my suffering.

Zipporah: No, Job! Don't fight your world. Don't question it. It's too big. The world always wins. It has too much power. [*Reflectively.*] You've always been a seeker, though. I've often wondered why you couldn't be content like the rest of us. I mean with the answers we *do* have. But you've never been content with traditional answers, never satisfied with what others told you was the truth as they understood it.

Job: A man has to find his own truth. Another's truth, like another's cloak, never fits properly.

Zipporah: But I don't care any more about all your high and mighty ideas, your searching spirit, your intellectual integrity. I'm sick and tired of seeing the man I love with rotting flesh and running sores. If you take my advice, you'll curse God and die, you'll blaspheme him and let him take out his vengeance on you in death. Death can't be worse than this. Curse God and be done with this suffering madness. Life has whipped you, Job, admit it!

Job: No! Aren't you also saying take me out of *your* misery, too, Zipporah? The misery of having to see your loved one suffer? I know, my dear, that we never suffer our miseries alone.

Zipporah: How sensitive of you to notice!

Job: Somewhere, and at some time, we touch one another with our miseries. We can't live in a secluded life on this earth. Our elbows of misery rub against one another from time to time as mine have yours. Do not think that I have forgotten your misery, having to listen to our friends as they pass by and say, "Poor Job." You have a heavy burden to carry, too. Misery may not necessarily love company, but it always collects it.

Zipporah: Oh, come on, Job. Your disease must have touched your brain and made it soft. Yes, I hurt. But get to the point. Answer the question. What about it?

Job: Curse God and die? Turn my back on him now? Why? If I believed that God had done this to us I would. But I do not believe that God causes hurt, suffering, and pain except very indirectly in that he has made a world in which these things can take place. God is too big a God to wipe out a man, Zipporah! Everything gone and God to blame? No!

Zipporah: Then who under the blue heavens do we blame? Who pays the account, Job? Is there something wrong with God having to answer . . . ?

Job: [*Interrupts.*] If this is the kind of God our fathers Abraham, Isaac, and Jacob gave us, then he will be pronounced dead in the years to come. Man will not tolerate a vindictive, arbitrary God who strikes down and takes away without reason—and I mean a reason we can see, feel, touch and understand.

Zipporah: Reason? How under heaven can you speak of reason at a time like this? What possible reason do you have to serve God now, to be loyal to him now?

Job: That's the key question, Zipporah. Do I believe in him just because he has been good to me? Or, to put it another way, will I serve God for nothing in return? With nothing to show for my years of belief and service, nothing to show for my obedience, my love, my devotion, will I serve him still?

Zipporah: [*Sarcastically.*] Yes, sir. Job will. After all, he has a reputation to protect. Wellspring of great wisdom and obedience: Job, the faithful. [*Weeps.*] Rotting in his fidelity.

Job: Am I wrong? Don't we all expect certain things from God for our service? We are trading animals by nature. We give our loyalty, our devotion, our faith, and we want something in return. No, we *demand* something in return. Just watch the devotion of the average man if he thinks God has done him wrong, or short-changed him, or has given someone else more than he has.

Zipporah: [*Pleading.*] Job! Must you be an example to all men? Can't you just suffer? Does there have to be a lesson?

Job: Yes! Yes! When God is silent, when nothing exchanges hands, will we still be devoted to him? I have to answer that myself!

Zipporah: I know the answer, already, because I know you, Job. You will remain his servant, you will stay committed to him though you die in this bed of ashes and cinders and never know why. You will serve him for nothing in return.

Job: To a bargaining humanity that expects to *get* something when it *gives* something that probably doesn't make much sense. But it does to me.

Zipporah: No, it doesn't make much sense to me. Everything we have is gone, and there is no reason. You can't point your finger at a man and say, "You did it, you fiend! You brute, I'll kill you." There's nobody to blame but God. Blame him. Point your finger at him. Tell him, "I reject you and your world and my suffering." Tell him, Job.

Job: It's never our prerogative to accept or reject suffering. We can only respond to it. I can only choose my response, Zipporah.

Zipporah: You know what? I'd like to see him respond to suffering. I'd like to see God live in this world for awhile. I'd like to see him come to earth and live like you and I are having to right now. I'd like to see a disappointed God. I'd like to see how God would handle his ash heaps. One who would know what it means to lose a friend, to love and not be loved in return, to suffer real physical pain like yours, Job. Answer me honestly. Do you think he would come?

Job: He might . . . if there was a reason.

Zipporah: He has a reason.

Job: What reason?

Zipporah: To show me that what I have to live with each day he can live with, and what's more, can make sense out of it, can handle it, Job—handle it like a God should.

Job: He could handle it, Zipporah.

Zipporah: No, I don't think so. I'm not sure God really understands what you're going through, and I want him to. *I* want him to know! Do you know what I would make him if I had my choice, Job? I'd make him a loving wife who had to watch her husband scratch his running sores, a wife who was helpless before it all.

Job: I know the feeling, Zipporah. But I believe he knows. Remember the psalm we used to sing together when the children were here?

> Whither shall I go from thy Spirit?
> Or whither shall I flee from thy presence?
> If I ascend to heaven, thou art there!
> If I make my bed in Sheol, thou art there!*

He knows, Zipporah.

Zipporah: I wish I could believe it. It makes all the difference in the world, Job. For if God has been through it all then he knows and he understands, and I can have hope through it all. If I just know that he understands and cares!

Job: I believe he is that involved with us.

Zipporah: No, Job. He's too far removed from us. God's not going to come down here, and he's not going to dirty himself on this earth and bother about towers that fall on innocent people—decent, respectable people or people slain by tyrants, or people like you, Job, who have their whole lives fall down around their knees. Answer me, Job. Do you think this God you're defending would really care that much?

Job: Yes. In your own skeptical, searching way you've found an answer, Zipporah. Not the whole answer, mind you, but a large part of it. I think God does care. That's what keeps me going. I'm not the kind of man to sit on an ash heap with a backful of stinking sores and all my life's work wiped out if I didn't believe that in spite of all this there is Someone in control of this world.

Zipporah: I wish I had your faith. But since I don't, I wish you would take my curse. Spit it at him and end it all, Job! That's still my advice.

Job: No. My answer is still no. When a man is on an ash heap there are two choices before him, two directions he can

* Psalm 139:7–8, RSV.

57

go. He can form a curse, or he can make a creed. A curse or a commitment. I've taken the latter. For better or for worse, that's my choice. You say he's the only one to blame. There's another way to see it. He's also the only one who can help—and he is the kind of God who will help us even if he does have to come to earth to do it!

For the first time in my life I felt that chasm in the bottom of my heart beginning to fill up. That hollow, hungry feeling began to disappear. I had to hear more. So I took an awful chance. I reached out and grabbed him. I was trembling and I guess I must have frightened him. Tears were streaming down my cheeks and Elizabeth said my eyes were about to pop out of my head. . . . I took him and said, "Mister, I've been looking for this all my life. Don't leave me now. Stay with me a few days and help us." And do you know, David, he walked right down into our village—and he a Jew—and he stayed.—Hasif, the Samaritan

Rescue on the Road

The Pharisees heard that Jesus was winning and baptizing more disciples than John. (Actually, Jesus himself did not baptize anyone; only his disciples did.) When Jesus heard what was being said, he left Judea and went back to Galilee; on his way there he had to go through Samaria.

He came to a town in Samaria named Sychar, which was not far from the field that Jacob had given to his son Joseph. Jacob's well was there, and Jesus, tired out by the trip, sat down by the well. It was about noon.

A Samaritan woman came to draw some water, and Jesus said to her, "Give me a drink of water." (His disciples had gone into town to buy food.) The Samaritan woman answered, "You are a Jew and I am a Samaritan—how can you ask me for a drink?" (For Jews will not use the same dishes that Samaritans use.) Jesus answered, "If you only knew what God gives, and who it is that is asking you for a drink, you would have asked him and he would have given you living water." "Sir," the woman said, "you don't have a bucket and the well is deep. Where would you get living water? Our ancestor Jacob gave us this well; he, his sons, and his flocks all drank from it. You don't claim to be greater than Jacob, do you?" Jesus answered: "Whoever drinks this water will get thirsty again; but whoever drinks the water that I will give him will never be thirsty again. For the water that I will give him will become in him a spring which will provide him with living water, and give him eternal life." "Sir," the woman said, "give me this water! Then I will never be thirsty again, nor will I have to come here and draw water." "Go call your husband," Jesus told her, "and come back here." "I don't have a husband," the woman said. Jesus replied: "You are right when you say you don't have a husband. You have been married to five men, and the man you live with now is not really your husband. You have told me the truth." "I see you are a prophet, sir," the woman said.—*John 4:1–19*

The woman said to him, "I know that the Messiah, called Christ, will come. When he comes he will tell us everything." Jesus answered, "I am he, I who am talking with you."—*John 4:25–26*

Then the woman left her water jar, went back to town, and said to the people there, "Come and see the man who told me everything I have ever done. Could he be the Messiah?" So they left the town and went to Jesus.—*John 4:28–30*

Then a certain teacher of the Law came up and tried to trap Jesus. "Teacher," he asked, "what must I do to receive eternal life?" Jesus answered him, "What do the Scriptures say? How do you interpret them?" The man answered: " 'You must love the Lord your God with all your heart, and with all your soul, and with all your strength, and with all your mind' and, 'You must love your neighbor as yourself.' " "Your answer is correct," replied Jesus; "do this and you will live."
But the teacher of the Law wanted to put himself in the right, so he asked Jesus, "Who is my neighbor?" Jesus answered: "A certain man was going down from Jerusalem to Jericho, when robbers attacked him, stripped him and beat him up, leaving him half dead. It so happened that a priest was going down that road; when he saw the man he walked on by, on the other side. In the same way a Levite also came there, went over and looked at the man, and then walked by, on the other side. But a certain Samaritan who was traveling that way came upon him, and when he saw the man his heart was filled with pity. He went over to him, poured oil and wine on his wounds and bandaged them; then he put the man on his own animal and took him to an inn, where he took care

of him. The next day he took out two silver coins and gave them to the innkeeper. 'Take care of him,' he told the innkeeper, 'and when I come back this way I will pay you back whatever you spend on him.'" And Jesus concluded, "Which one of these three seems to you to have been a neighbor to the man attacked by the robbers?" The teacher of the Law answered, "The one who was kind to him." Jesus replied, "You go, then, and do the same."—*Luke 10:25–37*

[*There is a knock at the door.*]

David: Yes. Who is it? Come in.

Hasif: Good morning, my friend. I wanted to drop in and see how you're doing.

David: [*Offended.*] Well, what . . . who are you? I don't know you. And besides, you look like . . . Are you by chance a . . . a . . .

Hasif: A Samaritan? Yes, my friend. Let me introduce myself. Hasif. Hasif, son of Bildad. And a Samaritan! Do I frighten you? I understand. Perhaps you are still a bit jumpy from your experience last week.

David: My experience? How did you know?

Hasif: Ah! I see the innkeeper has not told you. Very simple. I know because I found you on the road last week; I brought you here and paid the innkeeper to take care of you.

David: You rescued me? You saved my life! [*Pauses, then continues haltingly.*] I'm . . . sorry . . . about my reception of you, I mean. Please, sit down. I'm ever grateful. Now I understand. That's why the innkeeper would not tell me who brought me here. I kept asking him who made the rescue and he would just smile and say, "A friend." So you're the friend!

Hasif: Yes. He probably didn't tell you I was a Samaritan for fear you would have a relapse. [*Laughs.*] Knowing how you Jews feel about us Samaritans, I mean. But I see you're better.

David: Yes, indeed I am, thanks to you.

Hasif: [*Smiling.*] I thought so. There was a fear and anxiety in your eyes when I came in. [*Chuckles.*] I always say when a man is well enough to register fear and anxiety, he's on his way to health. By the way, you may call me Hasif.

David: My name is David. Please call me David. I suppose there's not much room for stiff formality when a man has saved your life, is there?

Hasif: Well, at least not with me. Tell me, David, how did you come to be in your plight? From your clothes I gathered you were a merchant—and a rather well-off merchant at that. Most of you rich merchants travel in caravans to ward off robbers. How was it that you were alone?

David: Well, I've had some time to think about that. I must confess in all honesty, Hasif. It was greed.

Hasif: Greed?

David: Yes. You are right. I am a merchant—and one of some means. I deal in fine cloth. You see, I was waiting for the arrival of some fine linens and silks from Damascus. You know the quality of their materials.

Hasif: Ah, yes. I've seen them in the homes of the rich. But I have owned them only in my fantasies.

David: Well, I was waiting for them to arrive so I could sell them to some of the merchants in Jericho. The caravan left the day before. I should have gone with them, but I desperately wanted those fine fabrics.

Hasif: I'm beginning to see what you meant by greed.

David: Anyway, I decided to let the caravan go, and travel to Jericho when the fabrics arrived. They came the very next day and I started off, hoping against hope that the robbers would not find me. So, you see, Hasif, it was love for that extra piece of silver that brought me to my plight. As it was, the robbers took my fine fabrics, my donkey, my money, my clothes, and beat me to within a hair of my life. [*Pauses.*] It's a miracle, Hasif. That I'm alive, I mean.

Hasif: Oh, it wasn't really that bad, David. You were bleeding badly, but once I got the bleeding stopped and got you to the inn, you were all right. There was no permanent damage that I—

David: No, Hasif, I mean it was a miracle that someone stopped, that someone cared enough to scoop me up. That's the miracle. I could have died by that road. There was no one on that road but you, Hasif. [*Pauses.*] Yet it seems I remember hearing footsteps near me once or twice. But I couldn't be sure. Everything was, and still is, so hazy.

Hasif: Well, there were at least two others on the road, David.

David: How do you know?

Hasif: There was a small group of us who stopped just outside the Jerusalem wall for a drink of water before we began our journey. There were a priest and a Levite at the well. From their conversation at the well, both were going to Jericho. The priest was in a hurry, and the Levite was waiting on someone, so the priest went ahead. The Levite's friend never came, so in a few minutes he struck out on the road, too. Those were the only two who left before me.

David: Well, maybe those were the footsteps I heard.

Hasif: It could have been. I stayed at the well and talked to several friends and then began my journey. We were all several minutes apart. The priest and Levite must have seen you. Those must have been the footsteps you heard. But why didn't they stop and help you?

David: [*Shaking his head.*] Their religion. *My* religion. That's why. If the priest had touched me he would have gotten blood on his hands and he would have been unclean for seven days. That means he may have had to miss his turn with the temple sacrifices.

Hasif: You mean he let a man lie bleeding, losing his life, so that he would not lose his turn in the temple ceremonies?

David: Probably. You have to understand, Hasif, the priests are awfully jealous of those turns in the temple. And the Levite—well, he probably thought I was dead. And if he had touched a dead man he would have been unclean and could not have done his duties in the temple, either. They couldn't help me because they were too religious. Funny how religion sometimes gets in your way in the attempt to do something religious—like help a man who's hurting.

Hasif: But, David, when you can't help a person because of your religion, and you can't accept him because of a doctrine, what good is it?

David: That's just the point! More and more I'm getting fed up with a religion that separates men and keeps them separated. Just like when you walked in. I categorized you right quick. You were a Samaritan. I was a Jew. I wanted you out of here before you even got in. I rejected you before I knew you. And you're the man who saved my life.

Hasif: No harm done, my friend. I have lived long enough—and as a Samaritan—to know about prejudice.

David: You understand, but that doesn't answer the questions about my religion. You know, my faith has a saying, "You must love the Lord your God with all your heart, and with all your soul, and with all your strength, and with all your mind, and your neighbor as yourself." That's a great saying, Hasif. I wish to God we would practice it. But you stopped. Now why would you, a Samaritan, stop to help me, a Jew? What's your religion, anyway?

Hasif: Well, it doesn't really have a name, exactly. It's got a Master, though. Named Jesus. He hails from Nazareth and I guess that's why I stopped.

David: Well, how did you meet him? Tell me about him.

Hasif: Well, it's a long story, David, and it calls for a confession. But I've saved your life and I guess you're obligated to hear my confession. [*Laughs.*]

David: Fair enough, Hasif. A life for a confession, any time!

Hasif: Well, it all started in the Samaritan village called Sychar. I was staying with a woman there. She was a beautiful woman. But she had a restless spirit. Nothing seemed to give her purpose and satisfaction with life. She had been married about five times and then I came along. Neither one of us wanted to commit ourselves to a marriage, so we stayed together, slept together, and lived together.

David: My religion looks down on that kind of arrangement. But I must admit it sounds convenient enough.

Hasif: Convenient, yes. But at the bottom of it all we both knew it was hollow and empty. Funny, though—I think we both felt that way, but we never talked about it. We skimmed the top off life. We never got below the surface. I think a lot of people probably live that way. Don't you? Well, anyway, one day Elizabeth—that was her name— went to the well for water. Jacob's well.

David: Ah, yes. I know it well. For us, a historic place, Jacob's well!

Hasif: Well, she went at noon because none of the other women went at that time and she wouldn't have to put up with those salty remarks and dirty looks. I guess you know how terribly pious and cold people can be.

David: Remember, I am a rich merchant. We have an old saying: "The very rich and the very poor are treated with the same scorn." I know. I know.

Hasif: Anyway, she went there and a Jewish man asked her for water. He played some kind of word game with her. He told her he had "living water" and she thought he meant spring water, or something. I never did get all the details straight. But then he told her to go call her husband. Elizabeth told him she wasn't married. "Right," he said, "you've been married five times and the man you're living with now is not your husband!"

David: And she had never seen him before? Strange, indeed.

Hasif: She asked him in a roundabout way if he was the Messiah and he said he was. She left her water pot and came running into the village screaming, "He's here, the Messiah is here, come see, come see." Well, I thought she had suffered a sun stroke—going to the well at noon like that —but when I got her in the house I could tell she was fine, just excited.

David: And who wouldn't be? I think it would be terribly exciting to meet a strangely mysterious person like that!

Hasif: Well, to make a long story short, a group of us went out to Jacob's well to see this man. I tell you, David, I've never before or since met a man like that man. He was kind and compassionate, and I felt like I could talk to him all day. His teaching was beautiful. He talked to us about eternal life and the way he explained it, it wasn't just living a long time, but it was an abundant, free, joyous, creative, and quality life.

David: I've not heard about this kind of life. Please tell me more!

Hasif: For the first time in my life I felt that chasm in the bottom of my heart beginning to fill up. That hollow, hungry feeling began to disappear. I had to hear more. So I took an awful chance. I reached out and grabbed him. I was trembling and I guess I must have frightened him. Tears were streaming down my cheeks and Elizabeth said my eyes were about to pop out of my head.

David: What happened?

Hasif: I took him and said, "Mister, I've been looking for this all my life. Don't leave us now. Stay with us a few days and help us." And do you know, David, he walked right down into our village—and he a Jew—and he stayed. And guess who he stayed with? Me and Elizabeth. That impressed me even more than his teaching. His acceptance.

David: I bet he gave you a good talking, too, though a man who believes like he does, I mean. I've heard some of these . . .

Hasif: [*Interrupts.*] No, David. He never preached to us, not once. It didn't seem to matter whether we agreed or disagreed with him, he would tell one of his parables and then just sorta step back and ask you to come to your own conclusion and share in his excitement with him. I knew from the way he talked and acted and the way he accepted and loved people that he must be the Master of life, the Messiah, as Elizabeth liked to call him.

David: He must have been an exciting person to have been around. What finally happened to him?

Hasif: Well, when he left two days later I went with him. But I had to leave Elizabeth, David, and I wept about this. I would lie out under the stars at night and I would cry. Not just because I missed her either. But because she didn't have what I had. If there's anything that hurts worse than leaving the one you love, it's seeing that one selling herself short, being less than what she can be.

David: You mean even though she called him Messiah she could not follow him?

Hasif: I know it sounds silly, but that's what happened at first. You know, David, it's one thing to believe in someone, but it may be another to really *accept* him. She just couldn't quite do it. Something was holding her back. Although the last time I saw her she had finally come around. He had become her Master, too. I guess there *are* some who can't accept him.

David: You know, Hasif, it's hard for human beings to cut loose the strings that hold them and really become free and joyous.

Hasif: Do I ever know that! It's being born again, a second time, and you have to clip the cord that holds you to those things that keep you from being free and loving like God intended and accepting people for who they are.

David: You've learned to put that into practice, Hasif. At least you did in my situation. But tell me, did you ever get back to the village, or did you just stay with this man? What happened?

Hasif: I stayed with him for three months. I can't begin to tell you how he stretched my soul, David. I thought so hard and he made me go so deep in myself that sometimes I would get sick at my stomach. For the first time in my life I began to care for people. Instead of stick men they became flesh and blood persons. When I saw them hurt, I hurt, and when I saw them die, a little of me died, too. And then that day last week . . . I saw you in the ditch.

David: And I'm glad you did.

Hasif: The ditch is where I lived most of my life, David. I know what to do with people when I find them there. That's my gift. And that's the story as to why I stopped to help you. He's the reason I stopped.

David: That's a beautiful story, Hasif. But the most amazing thing to me, a Jew, is that he could use people like you, an adulterer, a sinner.

Hasif: There are no others to use, David. Jesus used to tell us, "You are all sinners." And it never seemed to matter to

67

him whether the sin was sleeping with a mate not yours, or becoming prideful over *not* sleeping with someone else's mate. They were both sins to him.

David: Oh, I'm not sure I could go along with that, Hasif. I've always been taught that—

Hasif: [*Interrupts.*] But we've all sold out, David. I sold out to a woman, but you—you sold out to greed. And the priest and Levite? They sold out to becoming the caretakers of a sterile, fruitless religion that goes through forms without feeling and rituals without involvement. What's the difference? All these can eat up a man's insides and make him a slave.

David: Now that you've put it that way, I see your point. Or was that his?

Hasif: Oh, that was his!

David: [*Pondering.*] Ye-e-s-s! It's making more sense. Meaning and purpose in life. And never to sin again!

Hasif: No! I didn't say that. There is *forgiveness* for sin in this man, the Messiah, but that doesn't mean that we never sin again. I've had some terrible temptations since I've been a disciple of Jesus. And I've had some failures. But I always come back. I come back because I know he cares. There's nothing like having someone who cares to keep you straight. Just knowing—

David: [*Interrupts.*] Hasif, I want you to take me to this man Jesus. It's beautiful the way he's saved my life through you. I want to meet him and see what he has to say. A man with that kind of happiness and love!

Hasif: But don't expect that happiness and love all at once, David. He doesn't come to you just to give you salvation and make you happy. With his salvation there is commitment and with his happiness there is a prerequisite of knowing yourself and that means pain—at least it did for me.

David: But you've found happiness, I have seen it in your eyes, the way you've talked about him, your care for me.

Hasif: That may be, but Jesus didn't come—the way I understand him—just to make people happy. He came to teach us to become mature, growing, productive servants of God.

And sometimes this doesn't bring with it a spring-in-its-step happiness. It sometimes hurts to become that kind of person.

David: Regardless, I want to meet him. Take me to him.

Hasif: Stay in bed, David. When you're recovered we'll find him. I can find him. I know his habits. Anyway, I want to tell him about my saving your life. He'll be pleased about that. Maybe he'll even use it in one of his parables. Who knows? Anyway, I'll see you next week, David.

David: You'll be back and take me to him when I'm able to travel?

Hasif: That's a covenant. He'll be glad to see you. Good-by, friend. Or shall I say friend "in Christ"?

David: I think you might do that. Friend, friend "in Christ"! It just might be. Who can tell?

It's much clearer to me now, Peter. I was quite proud that my Christianity never interfered with my business, my social life, my politics. In my hiring and firing, buying and selling, in the bank vault and the voting booth my religion cut very little ice. Religion had its corner, categorized, catalogued, and separated from every part of life.—The man at the gate

---

Dialogue at the Gate

Jesus: "I have come in order that they might have life, life in all its fulness."—*John 10:10b*

Paul: "God is our Maker, and in our union with Christ Jesus he has created us for a life of good works, which he has already prepared for us to do.—*Ephesians 2:10*

Paul: "When anyone is joined to Christ he is a new being: the old is gone, the new has come."—*2 Corinthians 5:17*

Gatekeeper: Hello, there, friend. I've been watching you for some time. As a matter of fact, ever since you turned onto this straight, broad street. As I watched you shuffle along, did I detect a troubled mind and spirit? Your shoulders are sagging, your brow is furrowed, your head is heavy on your chest. I wonder: could I be of some help?

The Man: I doubt it. Nobody can help me now. I've just been before the Judge and the evidence for my case—and my chance of staying on *this* side of these gates—is being weighed now. And just think: I've always heard this was a happy place. Ha! Not for me. It *is* a beautiful place, though. We heard about it on earth, you know—how beautiful it was, and all.

Gatekeeper: Come! Sit here and talk with me. I have to stay near the gates for those seeking entrance, but I have time to listen. Would you like to talk with me and maybe lift some of that burden you're carrying around with you?

The Man: Yes, thank you. You're very kind. By the way, what do they call you?

Gatekeeper: Oh, I've been called many things: the unfaithful disciple—I left the Master during his trial; the "denying friend"—I denied him just like he told me I would. And, then, too, I've been called the Big Fisherman. You, of course, can see for yourself why they call me that. [*Laughs.*] I'm known by several other names, also, but you can call me by my most familiar name—Simon, Simon Peter. But now to you. Come, sit with me, and tell me why all the gloom.

The Man: Well, to put it bluntly, my trial went badly this morning, Peter. And it wasn't so much because of something I'd done—it was more what I had left undone. Do you know what I mean?

Gatekeeper: Oh, yes! Many have sat where you sit with the same feeling that something worthwhile had been left out of their lives.

The Man: Yes, that's it exactly. I kept the ten commandments to the letter. I was a good citizen, I went to church occasionally, and I gave—not too liberally—but I gave. Yet I evidently missed something splendid and beautiful along the way.

Gatekeeper: Do you know where you went wrong?

The Man: Well, it's hard to define, Simon. It's like trying to catch an evening breeze or describe the sunset. I know it's there—my mistake—but it's hard to pinpoint it!

Gatekeeper: Like trying to put into words the brush of a swallow's wing, isn't it? That's not mine, by the way. John used to say that all the time.

The Man: It's beautiful. And accurate. I was busy rummaging through my mind as I walked back from the Judgment

Hall. I think I may have a lead on what and where I missed a part of life. You know, Peter, I think I never really understood the meaning of eternal life.

Gatekeeper: I know the feeling. I've misunderstood so many things myself.

The Man: It's pitiful to admit it, and I hate to, but I've spent my whole life missing the meaning of something I thought I had understood. Think of it: going through decade after decade thinking you understand something you've never really understood at all!

Gatekeeper: Well, friend, that's one thing I've learned at these gates. Truth is limited to no age, and age doesn't necessarily guarantee depth of wisdom. How had you understood eternal life?

The Man: Well, I had always seen it as "everlasting life." I had always thought that if you believed in "the Master"—as you call him—that was sufficient. But from what the Judge said today, and from the way he scowled at me when I made my defense on this basis, I gathered there must be something more to eternal life.

Gatekeeper: Oh! Yes, there is more, considerably more. You've made a common error. You see, eternal life does mean "everlasting life," and it does have to do with the duration of life. But the eternal life spoken of by the Master also refers to the quality of life a person lives on earth.

The Man: Then he wasn't making statements just about the afterlife and heaven when he talked about eternal life?

Gatekeeper: No! It doesn't mean so much "living forever in heaven" as it does "living in depth on earth." This is what he meant when he said he came to give life and to give it more abundantly. This is what my good friend Paul meant when he said that if anyone was in Christ he was a "new creature." He had a new standard, a new quality, a new flavor to his life on earth.

The Man: I seem to remember the pastor of our church talking about Paul's idea of being "new" in Christ.

Gatekeeper: Oh, Paul was full of these ideas. They possessed him at times. He talked about being "created in Christ for good works," and "walking in newness of life" and being "alive in God" in the Master.

The Man: So if eternal life had to do just with the afterlife, Paul would not have mentioned this quality of life on earth?

Gatekeeper: Yes, my friend, eternal life means a lot more than just living a long time.

The Man: Man, I've been blind! I can see now that I actually used the concept of eternal life—of life with God here in heaven—as the way of taking the pressure off life on earth. I see it now! I sacrificed my conduct of the present to my hope in the future.

Gatekeeper: Well, like I've said before, you're not the first to make this mistake.

The Man: There's so much more to it. You're saying that eternal life is a quality of life and begins while we're still on earth, in relationship to our fellow-men, our jobs, our family, our total outlook on life?

Gatekeeper: That's right. You see, friend, I had to learn that the Master's idea of eternal life had much to do with my relationships on earth. Do you remember the story of Cornelius the Roman, told in the Book of Acts?

The Man: Yes, seems I remember it from Sunday school—or somewhere. Wasn't he the one you thought was not fit to be a Christian and you didn't want to go to him, or something like that?

Gatekeeper: That's close enough. What a lesson I learned that day. I found out that what I believed about my Master said something about what I *should* believe about this Roman captain. You know, I made the great confession at Caesarea Philippi.

The Man: I remember that: "You are the Christ, the Son of the Living God."

Gatekeeper: Right! But when I met Cornelius, that confession really made sense for the first time. I had to apply that confession to my relationships with my fellow-men. You see, I discovered that eternal life is easy to handle when you just catalogue it and save it for the afterlife. But it demands something when you see it as the Master meant it: a quality of life that begins on earth.

The Man: It's much clearer to me now, Peter. I was quite proud that my Christianity never interfered with my business, my social life, my politics. In my hiring and firing, buying and selling, in the bank vault and the voting booth my religion cut very little ice. Religion had its corner, categorized, catalogued, and separated from every part of life.

Gatekeeper: It's easy to do, my friend.

The Man: But why didn't I realize it? I couldn't see what was going on. I didn't recognize it. I thought I was a pretty good fellow.

Gatekeeper: Compared yourself with the folks about you?

The Man: Yes.

Gatekeeper: That always takes the edge off a man's desire to be better. If you stand tall in relationship to those about you, you're apt to be satisfied.

The Man: Ouch! I guess I've said that a dozen times in my life. "I'm as good as Mr. Jones and he's in church every time the doors open."

Gatekeeper: I know. And that's my point. If you're satisfied with yourself you don't do much soul-searching, and if you don't do much soul-searching you just don't grow, and without growth there's no quality of life.

The Man: Yeah, that makes sense. That's probably what happened to me. I just didn't put the emphasis on quality. [*Snaps his fingers as if an idea had just struck him.*] You know it may not mean anything, but I just remembered that playhouse I built for my little girl. I furnished it with second-hand furniture, hand-me-downs. I didn't even look for good furniture.

Gatekeeper: [*Quietly.*] The parable of the talents all over again.

The Man: What?

Gatekeeper: Nothing. Go ahead.

The Man: Well, that was all right for a playhouse, but I think I did the same thing with my soul. Oh, God! I'll never make it, Peter, and I've no one to blame but myself.

Gatekeeper: If I've said that about myself once I've said it a thousand times.

The Man: I never was concerned about having the best in my spiritual life. I put some shoddy things in my life: second-rate loyalties, and hand-me-downs in the form of traditions. I put my soul's security in believing that eternal life was only in the afterlife.

Gatekeeper: Now you know how I felt when I denied the Master and all the other foolish, impetuous actions I've cursed myself for a thousand times.

The Man: But to think, Peter, of the certainty I had that I was going to show up well in the books and accounts you were keeping on me.

Gatekeeper: Books? We were keeping? [*Laughs.*] Excuse me for laughing. I know you're sincere—foolishness usually is —but we don't keep accounts on people.

The Man: But I've always heard that—

Gatekeeper: No. You are your best account. A man is not known best by figures, pluses, minuses, big virtues, and little sins.

The Man: Then how do you know what he's—

Gatekeeper: [*Interrupts.*] He's known best by the quality of life he leads. If he wants to spend his life crying no to everything good, or being petty and small, fighting people, and in general missing all God's great yeses in life—it'll show, my friend, it'll show. No! We don't keep any records.

The Man: Well, how do you tell the quality of a man's life then, Peter?

Gatekeeper: Oh, there are dozens of ways. But two of the best are the way a man spends himself—the way he gives who he is—and the quality of faith he has.

The Man: Tell me more about this giving.

Gatekeeper: Let me ask you a question. How much did you give in your life?

The Man: You mean money, I guess. I've heard preachers talk about that. As a matter of fact it seems every time I went to church someone was talking about money. I went to find out how better to live life and the preacher was there talking about budgets. And you know—

Gatekeeper: [*Interrupts.*] No, no! Not just money. How much did you give of *yourself?*

The Man: That's a harder question. My checkbook stubs tell me how much money. But of myself! I don't know. I'll be generous to myself and say that at best I was less than a good Samaritan. I knew I couldn't bring anything with me, but I could never bring myself to truly give.

Gatekeeper: Any reasons why?

The Man: Oh, I don't know. I guess I felt like I was saving up for that big moment, that crucial issue, that most important event—but it never came. And I've wound up with a lot of "savings" on my hand. And I'm not talking about money either, Peter.

Gatekeeper: That's a familiar story. It's just like a man we had up here some centuries ago. He was a steward. His master had given him a talent—a considerable amount of money. But unlike his two colleagues, he was afraid to spend his, so he dug a hole, buried it, and thought he was a wise man.

The Man: I remember that one. When the master returned from his trip he took it from him and gave it to another man who had faith enough to spend his money wisely.

Gatekeeper: Right. And it does take faith to spend who you are and what you have. By the way, that's what I was mumbling about a moment ago.

The Man: Oh. Well, I'm afraid I've come up short in this giving idea. Maybe I've done better in the area of faith. Tell me about that.

Gatekeeper: The quality of a man's faith is one of the best ways to rate a man.

The Man: How do you figure that? I picked up an unspoken assumption in my early days with the church that faith was "believing what you know to be untrue."

Gatekeeper: Unfortunately that's the bill of goods a lot of people have bought.

The Man: What is a good quality faith? And how do you have faith in a world where a screeching car or mad dog, a virus the millionth size of a pinhead or a nail scratch can erase your name from the book of the living?

Gatekeeper: That's a difficult question. I had to answer it myself one day as I fled Rome's terrible persecution of us Christians. On my way out of the city I met the Master—or certainly the image seemed like him. He was headed into Rome and I asked him, "Quo vadis, Domine?" Oh, excuse me, you probably don't know Latin. That means, "Where are you going, Lord?" He replied, "To Rome to be crucified anew." I understood then what I had to do. I returned to Rome, withstood the persecution, and was crucified upside down.

The Man: That took faith!

Gatekeeper: Yes! Sometimes faith is best shown in a person's obedience to a duty he can't see, a cause he doesn't fully understand, a plan he hasn't conceived, tactics he can't personally accept.

The Man: I've often felt these descriptions applied to the church. Causes, plans, tactics—none of them ever crystal clear to me.

Gatekeeper: I know. We had the same problems in the early church. But we obeyed because we trusted the Master. We believed that he would work through us in spite of our mistakes. It's this kind of obedience that leads to—and maybe even comes from—a quality faith.

The Man: I would have liked to have had that kind of faith on earth. But I was so unsure of so many things when I was there.

Gatekeeper: A person is always unsure until he commits himself to something—or Someone. Commitment doesn't do away with insecurity, but it gives us the trust and the faith to move on regardless of our uncertainty. At least, this is what I found in my life.

The Man: I remember a quote I picked up somewhere that said: "Life is the art of drawing sufficient conclusions on the basis of insufficient evidence." And that takes faith!

Gatekeeper: Indeed it does. And not only faith like the world sees it, but that quality of faith that the Master taught.

The Man: Thank you, Peter. You've helped me to learn where I missed the greatest part of life. I'm due back at the Judgment Hall now. I hope it goes better than I expect. I've learned a lot. I hope it's not too late.

Gatekeeper: I hope not, too. Remember, God is more interested in what you learn than in when. After all, in his eternal eyes there is no when, only what. You've already paid the price of your foolishness. And it's never God's purpose just to punish. He wants to redeem and reclaim. The Master showed us that, you know.

The Man: Yes! Good-by, Peter. And thanks.

Gatekeeper: Good-by for now. I hope I shall see you again—soon.

Religious pride is the worst kind. And you know what it's composed of? One line, Amaziah, one line: "We thank you, Lord, that we are not as other men are. . . ." This pride stuffs a man's spiritual ears with wax; it covers his spiritual eyes with know-it-all scales; it hardens his heart with a cocksureness that's sickening. It takes away a man's ability to look into any new, unexamined corner of his heart. He can't even think except in certain patterns.—Amos

---

The Prophet and the Priest

Then Amaziah the priest of Bethel sent to Jeroboam king of Israel, saying, "Amos has conspired against you in the midst of the house of Israel; the land is not able to bear all his words. For thus Amos has said,

'Jeroboam shall die by the sword,
      and Israel must go into exile
      away from his land.' "

And Amaziah said to Amos, "O seer, go, flee away to the land of Judah, and eat bread there, and prophesy there; but never again prophesy at Bethel, for it is the king's sanctuary, and it is a temple of the kingdom."

Then Amos answered Amaziah, "I am no prophet, nor a prophet's son; but I am a herdsman, and a dresser of sycamore trees, and the Lord took me from following the flock, and the Lord said to me, 'Go, prophesy to my people Israel.'

"Now therefore hear the word of the Lord.

You say, 'Do not prophesy against Israel,
      and do not preach against the house of Isaac.'

Therefore thus says the Lord:

'Your wife shall be a harlot in the city,
      and your sons and your daughters shall fall by the sword,
      and your land shall be parceled out by line;
you yourself shall die in an unclean land,
      and Israel shall surely go into exile away from its land.' "

—Amos 7:10–17, RSV

[*There is a knock on the door.*]

Amaziah: Yes? Come in. Who are you?

Amos: I am Amos, prophet from Tekoa. You sent for me?

Amaziah: Ah, yes. The fig-picker from our neighboring state, Judah. Come in, come in. Indeed, I did want to see you.

Amos: And I wanted to see you, too.

Amaziah: Now what's all this I hear about your stirring up the people with these morbid and depressing prophecies? I even hear you have invited Assyria to come destroy us! As priest here at Bethel, I think it is my duty to find out just what you're after.

Amos: I've only come to—

Amaziah: [*Interrupts.*] And I think you should know, I've informed King Jeroboam that you're disturbing the holy place. This is the king's sanctuary, you know, Amos. It's dangerous to speak the way you do in the king's sanctuary.

Amos: I've come simply to proclaim God's word to you and your people, Amaziah. There is a lot of "religious" unrighteousness going on. And I'm surprised that you, the priest of God and the shepherd of the people, close your eyes to this, this abomination.

Amaziah: Now, wait a minute, Amos. We've got a good thing going here at Bethel. Why, the altars are crowded, attendance is good, and we've got more people sacrificing than ever before. The program is really going great. And I'll tell you something, Amos, we don't need a prophetic boat rocker now. Let the people alone; don't disturb them.

Amos: I can't leave them alone, Amaziah. There's a lack of true religion here. The people—

Amaziah: A lack of religion? You're out of your mind, Amos. Check the altars, check the assemblies. Man, just last week we had to put on another corps of Levites as custodians to keep things cleaned up. We're successful, Amos. Just come over here and look out the window and you'll see the crowds.

Amos: I said *real* religion, Amaziah. You've confused religious activity with religion. They've never been the same. I'm talking about a religion of the heart and mind, one that makes a difference in how a man lives; one that cares how he makes his living and how he does his living.

Amaziah: Please, Amos, spare me a lecture on theology.

Amos: You've asked me about my concerns. I'm telling you, that's all. I'm concerned about a religion in the courts, in the politics of the day, in the money-changers, the merchants, the laborers. What about *that* kind of religion, Amaziah?

Amaziah: Oh, for heaven's sake, be practical, Amos. You can't reach men with that kind of message. You know what people want in a prophet. They want a man who's serious but not solemn; they want a man who has been around and isn't naïve, but they don't want him to let them know it; they want a man who is wise but not too smart.

Amos: You have a clever way of spelling compromise, Amaziah.

Amaziah: You know as well as I that a smiling piety is more soothing than all the questions you've been raising, Amos. I have tried to get men to keep the rules and to do right things—

Amos: But what about their *being* right, Amaziah? What about the bribes in the courts, the short-changing methods going on in the sanctuaries; the shoddy sacrifices. A man's not religious if he sacrifices a fat calf in the morning and then sells a poor man into slavery in the afternoon because the poor creature can't pay for a pair of sandals.

Amaziah: Ah, come on, Amos, what's your point? Why all this holy noise about the way men live? What do you want from us?

Amos: Genuine righteousness, Amaziah, genuine righteousness. You've made religion the keeping of a thousand rules, a sacrifice at the proper time, but you've failed to teach a man that these rituals are acceptable only if he is honest with God and his fellow-man.

Amaziah: But if a person comes to the altar—

Amos: [*Interrupts.*] It's not coming to the altar that makes a man religious. It's not even the profession or the vow a man makes toward God. It's how he lives. You stifle the people with all this legalism. And I ask you, Amaziah, for all their "keeping the rules," are they any closer to God?

If religion doesn't bring a man closer to God it's not worth much! And if a man can't get along with his neighbor, what good are a thousand perfect sacrifices?

Amaziah: Lecture, lecture, lecture! Have I been through all my priestly training to be given ethical lectures by a fig-picker from Tekoa? By the way, is everything perfect in Tekoa? What about Judah? Is everything well there? Isn't there any corruption down south?

Amos: I'm sorry you took my words as a lecture, but—

Amaziah: [*Interrupts.*] Why have you felt compelled to come all the way up here to preach to us on how we ought to live? Charity begins at home, Amos. And so does perfection —and this bothersome stuff you call "righteousness."

Amos: Don't change the subject, Amaziah. I feel God called me here. I don't know why. I'm not perfect and neither is Judah—nor Tekoa. But their sins aren't going to get you off the hook. I didn't want to come here. I'm no prophet. I'm not even a son of a prophet.

Amaziah: [*Sarcastically.*] You make noises like a prophet. You chastise like a prophet. You raise your voice like a prophet. How can it be that you are not a prophet?

Amos: I mean I have no heritage to uphold, nothing at all to prove.

Amaziah: Oh, for God's sake, go back home, Amos. We're all right. Sure, things are wrong, but a lot of those who make money illegally put some of it into the sanctuary offerings. It all works out in the end. And there's one thing you seem to have forgotten, Amos. We in Israel are in God's covenant. Nothing's going to happen to us.

Amos: That's just the point. You think you have God's covenant. I am a fig-picker, as you called me, and I've learned you can always tell a tree by the kind of fruit it bears. God's people live by God's covenant. The covenant of God is a two-way street, Amaziah.

Amaziah: Well, we're living by those standards, Amos. We have all the feasts, all the sacrifices, all the programs. We go right by the book. We don't—

Amos: You blind fool—!

Amaziah: Careful, Amos, you're talking to man of God!

Amos: Then in God's holy name, act like it! Think like a man of God. Didn't you learn in your priestly training that religion is a thousand things more than just coming to the sanctuary on the Sabbath and going through holy acts?

Amaziah: I've already told you. No more lectures!

Amos: Religion has to make a difference in the way a man lives, Amaziah.

Amaziah: I'm not so concerned about how a man lives away from the sanctuary, just so he does his sacrifices.

Amos: God is displeased with this.

Amaziah: Why? Why does religion have to raise so many bothersome questions? You've come up here and challenged everything. Things are going well; I'm not going to make religion controversial!

Amos: Ah! Have you noticed, Amaziah, that whenever religion threatens a man's self-interest it suddenly becomes controversial? Tell a man God loves him and that religion is comfort. But tell that same man that because God loves him he must stop cheating his brother and that same religion becomes controversial.

Amaziah: There are laws that—

Amos: [*Interrupts.*] Tell a man that he can pray to God and religion is a comfort. Tell that same man he must speak the truth to his neighbor, even when it costs him money, and that religion suddenly becomes controversial.

Amaziah: But if you keep people stirred up all the time you—

Amos: [*Interrupts.*] Tell a man God loves all men and that religion is beautiful. But tell that same man that men of a different race can come to his sanctuary to worship his God, and that religion is controversial.

Amaziah: But Israel is God's chosen—

Amos: [*Interrupts.*] Tell a man God gives because of his grace, and that religion is "open arms"! Tell that same man God has made him a steward of those gifts and expects him to return some to God, and that religion becomes a "clenched fist."

Amaziah: I don't care what you say. We're all right. We're safe. God's going to take care of us!

Amos: Regardless of how you live before him and fail to serve him?

Amaziah: Yes!

Amos: [*Prays, looking upward.*] Oh, my God, how your prophet has grown to hate this secure smugness. The people are at ease, O God. They lie upon their beds of ivory and stretch out on their couches. They eat the fattest lambs out of the flock and take the choicest calf from out of the stall. They have nothing to do with themselves, so they lounge around composing trivial ditties and they have so much wine they have to drink it from bowls.

Amaziah: [*Interrupts.*] But you have given us the minds to secure wealth—

Amos: And they've forgotten you, O God. [*To Amaziah.*] You think everything is set up for you just because of an ancient covenant? A covenant you haven't kept? It's clear to me now, Amaziah, your religious activities have become a substitute for growth, for justice, mercy, faith, love.

Amaziah: Not so! We are God's people here! And we are proud of it.

Amos: You know, Amaziah, I've learned one thing in my preaching up here: religious pride is the worst kind. And you know what it's composed of? One line, Amaziah, one line: "We thank you, Lord, that we are not as other men are.

Amaziah: Is there no validity in being God's chosen?

Amos: It's pride over being chosen that I'm talking about. It's a pride that stuffs a man's spiritual ears with wax; it covers his spiritual eyes with know-it-all scales; it hardens his heart with a cocksureness that's sickening. It takes away a man's ability to look into any new, unexamined corner of his heart.

Amaziah: [*Exasperated.*] Suddenly, being the chosen of God is our sin!

Amos: No. You miss the point. You seem to think that being his chosen people exempts you from all sin. You know, the people were really amen-ing me while I was judging Damascus, Tyre, Edom, and the others. But as soon as I got to Israel there was a strange silence. Their warmth turned cold, their attention failed, their amens stopped. They haven't heard me yet, Amaziah. They haven't heard me because my message is different from yours. You've lulled the people to sleep. Your religion is dead, Amaziah.

Amaziah: But there's so much going on.

Amos: Worthless forms. The soul of your religion is dead. In the name of God it fastens dead weight upon progress; it opposes the discovery of truth; it stands as the arch-champion of things as they are. You have an institutional, dogmatic, antisocial, unrighteous religion.

Amaziah: Enough of this! You anger me! I'll have you thrown out.

Amos: The truth hurts only when it should, Amaziah. It seems that you have remembered God's election and forgotten repentance.

Amaziah: I am waiting for the Day of Yahweh. When God comes—

Amos: [*Interrupts.*] Ha! In your religious condition you want God to come? That reminds me of the day I was running from a lion and just as I topped a hill I ran head-on into a big black bear. That's what you're asking for.

Amaziah: No, you're wrong. The Day of Yahweh means—

Amos: [*Interrupts.*] The Day of Yahweh used to mean that God was coming to defeat his enemies. But now Israel is one of his enemies, and that destruction is for you, too. And you don't even recognize it. [*Pauses.*] Amaziah, you used to be a better man than this. Your reputation used to be sterling. Recently, though, it's all changed. What happened to you?

Amaziah: I don't know. There may be some merit in what you say—not that there is, but there may be. Those words about repentance— And righteousness— [*Reflectively.*] I can remember when I used to talk that way.

Amos: Can you change?

Amaziah: No. I can't change now, Amos. It's too late. I'd have to take back too much of what I've said and done. The people would laugh at me. It would be like starting over. It would mean getting a whole new set of values, starting out on another level of religious understanding. I guess

I'll be content to stay where I am. I'm willing to let religion remain a private affair between a man and God.

Amos: No, Amaziah, a man's religion is never private. Religion may be a personal affair, but it's never private. A man can't be superficial and a sham on his knees and be a saint on his feet. A man's religion is who he is, and that's never private. I know I'm lecturing again. But you know it's true, Amaziah. Religion and sin have never been a private affair between a man and God. They both have their social consequences.

Amaziah: Please go away, Amos. I'm tired and you've disturbed me. I can't bear your words. You've been too hard on me and my people. Go away. You haven't heard the end of this; the people won't hear you. They may even kill you. Soften your message, Amos, soften your message. Let up, let up!

Amos: I can't do that. I'll be back, Amaziah, I'll be back. And if the people rid themselves of me, there'll be another prophet. God will never leave the people without a prophet.

Amaziah: But what if he does, Amos?

Amos: He won't. He won't. He loves us too much. He'll raise up another prophet. And if that doesn't do it, God just may come himself.

Amaziah: To earth? What a dreamer you are, Amos. To earth? God?

Amos: Yes, to earth. He just may do that, Amaziah, he just may do that some day. He just may— He just may— [*Voice trails off.*]

*No! There's something else. I have to live it—not just with it,
but live it—and I cannot live what is not mine. Living with
what is not yours is like sucking on borrowed air, breathing with
somebody else's lungs, being kept alive by another man's heartbeat. And I can't live life that way. The things a man believes must
be his or he stands as a heretic in the faith he holds. This is what
is different about your faith. It isn't a faith in the law or the dozen
dogmatic doctrines of our people. Yours is a faith in a person. . . .
It's faith in you that has relieved me of the dry rot of tradition and
the deadening weight of spiritual conformity.—Nicodemus*

The Conversation Nobody Heard

The Pharisees and some teachers of the Law who had come
from Jerusalem gathered around Jesus. They noticed that some
of his disciples were eating their food with "unclean" hands—
that is, they had not washed them in the way the Pharisees
said people should.

For the Pharisees, as well as the rest of the Jews, follow the
teaching they received from their ancestors: they don't eat
unless they wash their hands in the proper way, nor do they
eat anything that comes from the market unless they wash it
first. And they follow many other rules which they have received, such as the proper way to wash cups, pots, copper
bowls, and beds.

So the Pharisees and the teachers of the Law asked Jesus,
"Why is it that your disciples do not follow the teaching
handed down by our ancestors, but instead eat with unclean
hands?" Jesus answered them: "How right Isaiah was when
he prophesied about you! You are hypocrites, just as he wrote:

'These people, says God, honor me with their words,
   But their heart is really far away from me.
   It is no use for them to worship me,
   Because they teach man-made commandments as though
      they were God's rules!' "

And Jesus said, "You put aside the commandment of God and
obey the teachings of men."

And Jesus continued: "You have a clever way of rejecting God's law in order to uphold your own teaching! For Moses commanded, 'Honor your father and mother,' and, 'Anyone who says bad things about his father or mother must be put to death.' But you teach that if a person has something he could use to help his father or mother, but says, 'This is Corban' (which means, it belongs to God), he is excused from helping his father or mother. In this way you disregard the word of God with the teaching you pass on to others. And there are many other things of this kind that you do."—*Mark 7:1–13*

It is late in the evening. Darkness has long since descended on the city of Jerusalem with the gentleness of a mother dove approaching her nest. The city is quiet except for those hollow night sounds that seem to bounce off the gates into the open hillsides. The shuffling feet of a forgotten beggar; the occasional cry of a human voice raised in fear, or maybe in unbridled joy; the soft murmurings of contented families in the safety of their homes are the only sounds that drift into the streets of the Holy City.

In one small, unpretentious house at the edge of the city a light burns brightly from the square-shaped window. A man sits quietly by a crudely made table. His head in his hands, he seems to be in deep thought.

In the distance there comes the distinct click, click, click of leather sandals on the cobblestone street. The step is deliberate, sure, purposeful. A man of some means and dignity emerges from the shadows and stops at the house. He pauses a moment before the door and then knocks quickly and quietly.

The reflective man on the inside rises and swings open the door. The two men look at one another for a moment and the host speaks first.

Jesus: Nicodemus, Nicodemus, how good to see you. Come in, come in.

Nicodemus: Thank you, Jesus. I hate to disturb you, but I had to see you. Simon Peter told me you were here in Esdras' house. He said that Esdras had to leave the city and had given you his home for a few days.

Jesus: Yes, Esdras is a kind man. This saves me the trip to Bethany every evening. Although Mary, Martha, and Lazarus are kind to keep us, it is better when I can stay in the city. I sent my disciples away tonight. I want to be alone. I have much to think about.

Nicodemus: Then I'm interrupting your meditation. I can come again—

Jesus: No, no, it's good to see you, Nicodemus. I have often thought about our conversation that night when you became one of my followers. Remember? "God so loved the world," I said, and you replied, "That's the kind of God I want." I haven't seen you since then. Tell me, what brings you here tonight?

Nicodemus: I've come out of concern for you, Master. I'm disturbed. Some of the leaders and elders are beginning to gather some strength against you. It looks grave to me. You mean much to my life. You are, indeed, my Master. I don't like what I hear and see. I was doubtful about coming. I feared someone might see or hear me.

Jesus: Don't be concerned, Nicodemus. This is a conversation no one shall ever hear. Sit down now, and tell me what you have heard, my friend.

Nicodemus: Well, there is much confusion. Consternation has spread among the Pharisees and scribes and has even come into the ranks of my body, the Sanhedrin. Your teaching seems to be causing the most stir and trouble.

Jesus: Is it my method that has offended my brothers?

Nicodemus: Oh, no, your method is orthodox enough, but what you say is creating chaos. The other day in one of your parables you made it clear that it was not the Gentiles but the unrepentant Israelites who were hindering the coming of the Kingdom.

Jesus: You are, no doubt, referring to the time when I taught that the hard, unrepentant ones are not among the "sinners" as we know them, but among the "righteous," those who are most religious?

89

Nicodemus: Exactly. You have made acceptance by God unconditional.

Jesus: So I have. I believe the Scriptures reveal this. The prophets are full of these ideas. What else?

Nicodemus: Well, the scribes say that now the law is of only token importance. You must understand our point of view. The law has been our whole life; in our every teaching it's exalted; we have known nothing but the law in our spiritual lives.

Jesus: I know. Now I have mocked the law, slain your traditions, and even reinterpreted who the Messiah is.

Nicodemus: Yes. Now understand, Master, I believe in you. That's why I've come. The people are anxious. There's talk in the streets—

Jesus: There's always talk in the streets, Nicodemus. People are never easily led to anything, even to the Kingdom of God. Our history is filled with this. Moses had his grumbling, whining people who were dissatisfied with the insecurity of their freedom—and freedom is always insecure, Nicodemus. They wanted to go back to molding bricks and enjoying the fruits of Egyptian prosperity.

Nicodemus: If we could only have the faith of Abraham!

Jesus: Well, even Abraham was no doubt called a fool by his contemporaries for leaving his wealthy place and moving toward an unknown land. Joshua, Isaiah—

Nicodemus: [*Interrupts.*] Micah, Amos, Hosea—they all had a difficult time getting God's truth to God's people.

Jesus: Sometimes, Nicodemus, I want to stand on the hillside and shout to this city, those "holy" people, "Don't you know when God is speaking to you?" And at other times I just want to cry. Does it surprise you that the Son of Man would cry?

Nicodemus: No, Master, not when one so perfect sees so much imperfection.

Jesus: It's the same today as it has always been. People will not hear unless they want to hear—it's all in the will. They won't accept me as Messiah unless they will to. But come now, be more specific, what else are they saying about me?

Nicodemus: Well, you know how people are. Some of the

leaders don't like where you go or the people you run with. You'll have to admit, it's not very becoming for a rabbi of your standing to be found with sinners. And when you forgave that adulteress, you should have seen those leaders! They strutted and blew about that for days. Some of the scribes still haven't recovered. You must remember that we have to keep ourselves unspotted—

Jesus: No! I've said it before and I'll probably have to say it a thousand times over: the sick need the physician, not the well. That's the problem with our world today, Nicodemus. The "physicians" are on one side keeping themselves "unspotted," and the sick are on the other side getting sicker. And I'm trying to get them together.

Nicodemus: I understand that, Master—

Jesus: [*Interrupts.*] And anyway, I didn't come from my Father to please these whitewashed tombstones, these hypocritical wind-bags, these holier-than-holy, doctrinaire legalists.

Nicodemus: I honestly think those kinds of names have not endeared you to them, either. [*Smiles.*]

Jesus: I came to heal men—all men, even *these* men. Pleasing and healing—they are not the same, Nicodemus.

Nicodemus: I know. Sometimes there's displeasure in the healing process. Pain, discomfort, inconvenience.

Jesus: Yes, I came to give men a more abundant life. But perhaps I have to convince them first of the inadequacy of the life they have now. Sometimes it seems to be a losing battle. What else are they saying?

Nicodemus: Well, they seem to think that you enjoy yourself too much. Frankly, you didn't come off too well at the wedding feast in Cana of Galilee. That only got you a reputation as a winebibber and a fun-lover. You'll have to learn how to take life more seriously. And those disciples you have. My! It seems you could have selected a bit more discreetly.

Jesus: Yes, I wish I could have. Heaven knows, I have to repeat myself to some of those men a thousand times to be understood, especially to that Simon Peter. My! But there are two redemptive things about these men, as crude as they are.

Nicodemus: Yes, there must be something I haven't seen. They *are* crude!

Jesus: Their minds are clear; they have not been shackled by tradition and fettered by the past. And they have the ability to commit themselves. And that's what I must have above all else, Nicodemus. I need men who will say yes and no and stick by it. I would willingly trade ten thousand scribes and Pharisees for ten men who are open to the truth of my good news. And what about you, Nicodemus. Who do you say that I am?

Nicodemus: You are the truth. I've already told you, I believe in you. As I told you before, my life has been one long search for the truth.

Jesus: Why, Nicodemus? Why search and seek? Why not follow the tradition of the priests, elders, or your own Sanhedrin? It's all set. There's nothing required of you but assent to what they say you believe.

Nicodemus: But, Lord. I—

Jesus: [*Interrupts.*] It's all written down in the Talmud. All you have to do is to believe it, to perpetuate, say it's yours, take it.

Nicodemus: No! There's something else. I have to live it—not just with it, but *live* it—and I cannot live what is not mine. Living with what is not yours is like sucking on borrowed air, breathing with somebody else's lungs, being kept alive by another man's heartbeat. And I can't live life that way. The things a man believes must be his or he stands as a heretic in the faith he holds. This is what is different about your faith. It isn't a faith in the law or the dozen dogmatic doctrines of our people. Yours is a faith in a person.

Jesus: You have learned well, Nicodemus. I'm pleased with you. Faith in a person.

Nicodemus: This is what you meant when you told me last time, "Whosoever believes in *me*—" Not books, or laws, or doctrine, but you, Master, you! That's the only kind of faith that has zest and spirit. It's faith in you that has relieved me of the dry rot of tradition and the deadening weight of spiritual conformity.

Jesus: Ah! You've truly taken root, haven't you, Nicodemus?

92

Nicodemus: Ah! My father would die a dozen deaths if he could hear me talk this way. He always wanted me to be a good Israelite. And to his mind, being a good Israelite meant raising no more questions than you had answers.

Jesus: Yes, Nicodemus, you are right. Unfortunately life is not wrapped up in neat little packages like that. It is composed of illness, death, paradox, hatred. And I have come to teach the way, to speak the truth, to give the life to men in this kind of world. I want men to have life at its best, its fullest, its finest. I want—

Nicodemus: Excuse me for interrupting, Master. But I have a serious question about all of this. I know what you're here to do, what your purpose is. And I understand you. I accept you. But I wonder if the people are ready for you—yet?

Jesus: What do you mean, Nicodemus? The people?

Nicodemus: I'm not sure we understand your parables, your teachings, your concepts. Maybe they're too far over our heads. Maybe we aren't ready. For example, your Sermon on the Mount. Do you think the people really understood all of that?

Jesus: I should hope so. I put hours of thought and years of preparation on some of those sayings. I hope they understood.

Nicodemus: No! They'll misconstrue it, hear what they want to hear, like you said a few minutes ago. Men have a way of taking truth and cutting it up, watering it down to fit their own needs. I'm sorry. But I wonder if we are ready for you?

Jesus: Is my Father a fool, Nicodemus? Has he failed in his judgment of the people of history? When will men be ready for the truth about life, Nicodemus? When? When? I'll tell you when. Never! My Father made men free. That was a terrible risk, Nicodemus, because a free man can go his own way instead of the way his creator would like for him to go.

Nicodemus: That seems to have been our history thus far. Why?

Jesus: Man takes the easy road, Nicodemus—seldom the

93

"truth" road in his life. The road of truth is narrow, it's rocky, it's unattractive many times. No! Men will never be ready for truth. Men have to have truth thrust before them; few go in search of it. I can only hope that they will see it when it is set squarely before them.

Nicodemus: God has been preparing men for centuries for your coming. Moses, Abraham, the prophets, the writings, the law. If men are not ready, what a sickening waste of history. All those years down the drain, lost. And tens of thousands of broken hearts for you and your Father. Maybe you're right, Jesus.

Jesus: About what, Nicodemus?

Nicodemus: The most difficult thing in the world is to tell your people all the truth when they've been used to seeing and hearing only a part of it, and when they've accepted that part they have seen as *all* of the truth.

Jesus: Yes, it's like looking through a dark, dirty glass. Suppose you're never able to go outside to see reality. All you know is what you see through the dirty glass. It's all you've ever seen. You grow accustomed to seeing the world through that glass and you think your world actually looks like that. You accept it. You just know that what you see and the way you see it is true.

Nicodemus: Then one day someone comes along and cleans the glass. Your whole picture of the world changes.

Jesus: What you saw, Nicodemus, wasn't wrong. It was just inadequate, incomplete, unclear, hazy.

Nicodemus: Yes, Master. That's what you've done. You've dared to clear the haze from the glass of men's souls and minds. But I wonder—do you think some men would prefer to remain half-blind to reality, to have their vision beclouded, to continue down that broad way of half-truth? If they want to remain where they are and not see things clearly, then, Master, you're in trouble.

Jesus: That's what you came to tell me, wasn't it, Nicodemus? I think I've known that from the beginning.

Nicodemus: You're in real trouble, now, because you have cleared the vision of men who have not wanted their vision cleared. You say, tell men the truth, and they'll accept it.

I say, tell them the truth, and you're apt to be stoned to death.

Jesus: That's a risk I have to take, Nicodemus.

Nicodemus: And that's the rub, isn't it, Master? You can have all the truth in the world but if you can't get men to accept it— Oh, if there were only some way to get your message across without rooting up the old paths, revising our laws, taking God out of his box in the holy of holies behind the veil.

Jesus: But there's not! Ecclesiastes was right, Nicodemus. There is "a time for every matter under heaven: a time to plant, and a time to pluck up what is planted; a time to break down, and a time to build up; a time to keep, and a time to cast away; a time to rend, and a time to sew." And sometimes you have to pluck up, and break down, and cast away, and rend before you can plant, build, keep, and sew. I cannot alter my course now.

Nicodemus: But, Master, if you'll just be practical—

Jesus: Practical? No one will ever know how much spiritual adventure, how much heavenly initiative, how much obedience to my Father has been stifled by that one plea: "Be practical."

Nicodemus: I'm only trying to help, Master. I do not wish to compromise you. I only want to be a good disciple.

Jesus: Then you must realize that discipleship is not always practical, Nicodemus. Amos' confrontation of Amaziah was not practical. Jeremiah's sermon on the Temple steps decrying the status quo was not practical. And my coming in flesh and blood is the most impractical thing we've ever done.

Nicodemus: But there must be a way besides—

Jesus: [*Interrupts.*] You stick with what's practical and you'll live an uneventful, pallid, fruitless life. That's what I meant when I said just the other day that I have come to give life and to give it with abundance. That means having something in your life that's "over the top," overflowing, full, spiritually exciting and exhilarating.

Nicodemus: All right, Master. If you refuse to be practical, then you had better look at some facts. I want to tell you

95

the kind of people you're dealing with. Don't think I'm presumptuous; but here are the people whom you're going to have to face in your ministry.

Jesus: You've lived long in this country, Nicodemus. I would welcome your understanding of the people as you see them.

Nicodemus: There are the spiritually ignorant who let the rest of society make up their minds for them. They are, for the most part, neutral on the crucial issues of life. And regardless of how much you try to convince them of what you are, they will still turn to their neighbors and say, when you've finished speaking, "What did he say, what did he mean, and what should I do about it?" These are the spiritual parasites. They live off what others tell them to believe.

Jesus: I have met many of these in my almost three years with you. Are there others?

Nicodemus: Yes, there are those who listen and understand but don't have the courage or the will—or perhaps both—to apply what they hear to their own lives. They leave your teaching, saying, "How fine that obedience, and commitment, and individual responsibility are—others ought to have more of these qualities."

Jesus: And what about those who want to be leaders, but whose vision is too narrow, whose knowledge is too limited; their way of looking at the world and "all that God made" is too small to fit the facts. You've had some of these in the Sanhedrin. They are frustrated and frustrating. Once they get an idea they cannot be swayed.

Nicodemus: Yes, but in all honesty, I must say that all our people aren't that bad. There is a group—a small one, it seems at times—who still has those childlike qualities: openness, honesty, the capacity to be taught. You said it so beautifully one day yourself: "Except you become as a little child you shall in no wise enter the Kingdom of Heaven."

Jesus: But I have a feeling you have not mentioned my worst enemies.

Nicodemus: You are right. The worst group you'll have to

deal with is the one composed of the leaders whose traditions decide the truth for them. They are amazingly like that first group that looks to others for their beliefs, except that this group looks to past thoughts, feelings, and attitudes.

Jesus: Ah, yes. These have dogged my heels and drained my energies since I began my ministry. They have taken so much from me.

Nicodemus: Now, Master, I don't want to frighten you, but I feel I must tell you. These are the ones who will kill you. And right now you're standing between them and their traditions.

Jesus: It is sad that I hear such words from such a faithful follower and loyal friend. I fear you speak the truth. Idolatrous traditions! They seem to be the problem.

Nicodemus: Yes, and as heaven is my witness, they love these more than God. You can say almost anything about God, but they'll kill you if you tamper with their cherished dogmas. They are concerned enough to become aroused, they are threatened enough to become anxious, they are just insistent enough to demand their own way. You're on a collision course with them.

Jesus: What have I done, Nicodemus? Have I not loved well enough? Have I not given enough of myself? What have I done?

Nicodemus: I may put it poorly, Master, but I think the real problem is that you love too innocently, too thoroughly, too completely. But mostly, too innocently. I'm not sure that guilty men can be loved like this and ever really understand it; and those who feel no guilt—the righteous ones who never know how much they have sinned—just don't care.

Jesus: My Father will appreciate the defilement of innocence. He has frequently spoken to me of the innocence in the Garden at the beginning of things and how—

Nicodemus: [*Interrupts.*] We men seem to have something against innocence. We deface and defile it wherever we find it. That's why I'm afraid for you. You are too innocent, too beautiful a man, and you love too well.

Jesus: But that's what love is, Nicodemus. The *will*, the *will* to love those who defile and mar the innocent. Only a love of the will can love an enemy. And if I have to die to show it, I'm ready. Love is in the will!

Nicodemus: What will you do if they do come for your life, Master?

Jesus: I'll give it to them.

Nicodemus: And then? Master, what then?

Jesus: And then I'll wait. I'll wait with a fervent hope and a profound prayer that my followers, like you, Nicodemus, will know what to do with a Lord who willed to love even to his death. And you, what will you do if they take my life, Nicodemus?

Nicodemus: There's only one thing to do, Master: to live by your example! That's all I can do. No! That's *everything* I can do. Good night, my Lord.

I think my real reaction has been the number of Christians in my experience who said they were converted but showed no change. I guess that, more than any other consideration, has made me suspect the whole matter of conversion. . . . I still have the picture of people coming down the aisle, shaking hands with the preacher and never showing any difference in their lives. That led me to conclude that conversion was unreal.—Rick

"A Sermon on Conversion?"

There was a man named Nicodemus, a leader of the Jews, who belonged to the party of the Pharisees. One night he came to Jesus and said to him: We know, Rabbi, that you are a teacher sent by God. No one could do the mighty works you are doing unless God were with him." Jesus answered, "I tell you the truth: no one can see the Kingdom of God unless he is born again." "How can a grown man be born again?" Nicodemus asked. "He certainly cannot enter his mother's womb and be born a second time!" "I tell you the truth," replied Jesus, "that no one can enter the Kingdom of God unless he is born of water and the Spirit. Flesh gives birth to flesh, and Spirit gives birth to spirit. Do not be surprised because I tell you, 'You must all be born again.' The wind blows wherever it wishes; you hear the sound it makes, but you do not know where it comes from or where it is going. It is the same way with everyone who is born of the Spirit." "How can this be?" asked Nicodemus. Jesus answered: "You are a great teacher of Israel, and you don't know this? I tell you the truth: we speak of what we know, and tell what we have seen—yet none of you is willing to accept our message. You do not believe me when I tell you about the things of this world; how will you ever believe me, then, when I tell you about the things of heaven? And no one has ever gone up to heaven except the Son of Man, who came down from heaven."—*John 3:1-13*

Rick: Man! Was I ever disappointed in that sermon yesterday, John. One of the reasons I chose you as my pastor and this as my church was that I felt you had more to say than that. Here we are in the most creative country in the world, and what do you talk about? Conversion! I heard enough of that when I was a kid.

John: Well, I'm sorry you didn't approve of the sermon, but I want you to know that I thought it was necessary. Even basic to our faith.

Rick: I just don't understand how an intelligent and keen pastor like you can say that. You keep up in our society. You know how much we've progressed. Look at our technical progress. Pills can put us to sleep and drugs can make us alert. Surgery is by laser beam. Organ transplants replace our worn-out instruments.

John: I know, Rick. I am familiar with the catalogue of progress. Contact lenses help us to see better and electronic watches keep us on time. Stereo gives us sound with dimension.

Rick: Well, it's true, John. We have the most affluent culture in the history of man. We are the sharpest-witted, best-dressed, wealthiest and most mobile people on God's earth.

John: You'd better take off those rose-colored glasses, my friend. We are all that you say. But that's only one side of the story. It's the other side that brings me restless nights. In Biafra, blacks destroy blacks and the children starve. In India, tens of thousands die each week and just as many more are born to begin the cycle of birth, hunger, starvation and painful death.

Rick: In Ireland, the most religious people there throw their bombs at one another and kill Christian brothers under the sign of the cross. And in Vietnam our tender young men not even out of adolescence are intimately acquainted with the smell of death and the shadows of fear.

John: But that's only the beginning. Our cities have been burned and bombed. We have white oppression and black rage. Some college campuses have a student population that has pushed centuries-old schools into chaos.

Rick: Now that's just my point, John. These are social issues and don't have anything to do with conversion. Conversion is personal.

John: I'm not sure I'll buy that, but let it stand for a moment and look elsewhere. What about the kind of people you and I are—and our fellow-men?

Rick: What do you mean?

John: What about those jealous feelings that are stirred when someone gets what we want? Or those secret lusts no one knows about but you—and God? Or that impatience that lashes out at our colleagues at work or anyone who might happen to be around as a convenient whipping boy? As a pastor I know the frequent errors of our "best" people.

Rick: But, John, it can't be that bad in the church.

John: Oh, no? I read recently a description of many church members. I've got it on the desk here if I can just find it. [*Pauses.*] Oh, yes. Here it is. Listen: "Sharp tongues that speak without facts, minds that are lame in understanding frustrating complexities, and spiritual pride that rejoices because it has not changed a thought in twenty years. People who wear a mask so tightly that there is little difference any more between them and their mask. They've grown together." Now, in the light of the evidence in our nation, our world, and our selves, let's talk about conversion.

Rick: I'm beginning to see the point. I hadn't seen it just that way.

John: Good. What I'm saying is very simple. Selfishness is alive. Hatred is prevalent. Justice is missing. Mercy is that which others ought to have toward us. Humility is what we like to see in other people. And love tends to become a syrupy sweetness that escapes the hard realities of life. Add all these together. There is one grand total, one ultimate conclusion. Sin is alive. And that, in a three-word sentence, is exactly why we need to speak about conversion.

Rick: This is important to you, isn't it?

John: It's basic to the Christian faith. God knows, we need changing. Even a superficial acquaintance with our world

101

shows that something is wrong. And conversion helps to remedy that something.

Rick: Well, I guess I tuned you out when I heard the word *conversion.* Give it to me slowly, John. How do you see it?

John: Conversion is change in a person. Sin breaks relationships with God and man. Conversion works to reconcile that brokenness, that splitness in our lives. We, like Paul, do what we don't want to do, and what we want so desperately we can't bring off. Conversion helps us to begin to reverse that process.

Rick: Now, you see? I've heard all that before! I still wonder if it's really necessary, John. I have trouble admitting its necessity.

John: I think it *is* necessary because it's a change on the inside of a person. There are only two ways to effect change in man's basic behavior. Legislate it from the outside, which calls for enforcement, or motivate it from the inside, which calls for discipline. Law does the former. Conversion does the latter.

Rick: I can see that. I think my real reaction has been the number of Christians in my experience who said they were converted but showed no change. I guess that, more than any other consideration, has made me suspect the whole matter of conversion.

John: Judge history, its institutions, and its movements by their best, Rick, not their worst.

Rick: Yeah, I know. But I still have the picture of people coming down the aisle, shaking hands with the preacher and never showing any difference in their lives. That led me to conclude that conversion was unreal.

John: That kind is unreal. When I talk about conversion I mean a complete change of mind, heart, and will.

Rick: Well, let's try it again, then. If you have something new I want to hear it. Where and how does it start?

John: Some will disagree with me, but I see it as a process. Paul called those in Christ new creatures, but none of us becomes a new creature instantly. To me, conversion begins with confession, an awakening, the honest admission that something is wrong. Something like we've done today in listing the errors and ills in our world and in ourselves. Do you remember the parable of the Prodigal Son?

Rick: Yes. He was the one who asked his father for his part of the inheritance, converted it to cash, and took off on his own, wasn't he?

John: Right. And after he had severed relationships at home and squandered his money, he found himself in a pig sty feeding a farmer's pigs. Not a very charming spot for a "man about town." The Scriptures tell us he "came to himself." That was his awakening. He saw it and "told it as it was" for the first time that it really mattered. He confessed that his life was a mess and that he needed something outside himself.

Rick: You know, John, if we are honest with ourselves, we all feel that need. I've felt it myself but I've had some real hang-ups with counterfeit conversion. I've repressed that need. I'm not sure God could have gotten through if he had wanted to.

John: Oh, I don't know about that. Don't ever count God out. He often comes in the most inopportune times and in the most out-of-the-way places. In Michelangelo's fresco *The Creation*, Adam is reclining, leaning on his elbow, hand hanging loose, lifeless. In sharp contrast, there is the finger of God an inch away, dynamic with power and life, ready to touch Adam with life. That's the way it is. In our most apathetic, complacent moment we can suddenly awaken to new life, new creation, resurrection. That is the new birth, the birth from above.

Rick: Does it always happen that way?

John: No, I don't think so. Conversion may be that time when God breaks in upon us. No, not quite. I think rather he has been there all the time and it is simply that we become aware of him and respond to his "already-thereness."

Rick: It's like in the science lab when you discover a law or a scientific relationship that's been there all along, only you didn't know it.

John: That's right. But conversion begins with the confession of the publican, "God be merciful to me, a sinner." It is to confess to God our sinful state, our inability to pull ourselves up by our bootstraps,

Rick: It begins with confession? Now that doesn't seem too difficult to me.

John: For many people it is.

Rick: Why?

John: There may be many reasons, but for us in America, one of the most powerful reasons is our comfort and affluence.

Rick: I don't understand.

John: We are still very Hebrew in the belief that righteousness and material prosperity, or sinfulness and poverty are intricately intertwined. To put it simply, it's the old idea if I'm good God will reward me, if I'm bad he will punish me.

Rick: Why, I was raised with that idea, John. Anything wrong with it?

John: As a matter of fact, there is. If we have little pain or suffering, then we are apt to have little self-reflection. Most of us don't think deeply about life until it's threatened.

Rick: What you're saying is that comfort and affluence do not foster examination.

John: Right. We tend to relate physical, material comfort as being a symbol of our spiritual well-being. This is often a false standard. This standard keeps us from confessing. We're doing all right materially, and that must mean that we aren't too bad; and if we aren't too bad, then there's no reason to confess.

Rick: I really came here for more of a discussion, but you've really got me interested in this idea now. Mind if I pick your brain some more?

John: No. Go ahead.

Rick: A moment ago you said conversion begins with confession. Evidently this is not the end of it all. What's next?

John: Again some will disagree, but to me conversion deepens with repentance. Repentance means to turn, to change direction, to begin to walk in another direction. Repentance decides to do something about sin other than just confess it. The prodigal son confessed it but he also climbed out of the pig sty and went home. His "coming to himself" was confession, his going to his father was repentance.

Rick: I'm afraid I've hung up on that word, too. I've heard repentance all my life. I'm not sure I can recall more than a dozen people who really demonstrated this change. Hypocrites!

John: Yes. And I am convinced that what makes more hypocrites today than anything else is confession without repentance.

Rick: I don't quite follow you, John.

John: Well, for instance, I once knew a jealous, nasty-spirited elderly lady. Nothing suited her. When I used to visit her she would say, "Oh, I know I should not be like this, I ought not to be so nasty." That was confession. But she died like she had lived. Bitter and hostile.

Rick: Oh, I get it. She had confessed but she had not repented.

John: Right. The best way I can put this idea is "intention put into action." It is to begin to practice what you profess. And right here repentance begins to fade into another element in conversion.

Rick: What is that?

John: Resolve. This is where conversion matures. The goal of conversion is to make us "new creatures." But there's nothing automatic about that initial experience with Christ. We don't become new creatures overnight. We don't change habit patterns instantly. When Paul responded to Christ on the Damascus road he went into Arabia for a long period of time to hammer out what kind of person he had to become.

Rick: I can't remember the "old time religion" ever saying much about resolve. If anything, this whole matter of Christianity was presented as easy and simple.

John: You are right in many instances. It is at this very point that some of our evangelism has fallen short. We have often declared that belief is easy. "All you have to do is to come down this aisle and believe."

Rick: That's what I mean. I've heard that since I was a kid. "Just believe."

John: No! Even the demons believe, says the Scripture. We have tended to make acceptance of Christ no more difficult than shaking the pastor's hand. What we have failed to stress is the resolve needed to become that new creature, that new man.

Rick: Then resolve is really the will to follow through with confession and repentance?

John: That's the way I see it. Beginning conversion without that resolve will often negate the entire experience. Resolve is in the will. A man is never changed until his will is changed. "Born againness" has to take place in the will of a person.

Rick: What does this resolve in the will mean in practical terms?

John: It means that you have to will to love that lout who gets under your skin. You have to will to love that smart-aleck youngster who so disgusts you with his love beads, smelly body, and dirty, stringy hair. And what many white churches have yet to learn is that we have to will to love that black man who comes to the church door with belligerence on his face, cynicism on his lips and bitterness in his heart.

Rick: Or the absentee landlord who lets his ghetto dwelling rot from under people while infecting them with diseases carried by rats, roaches and other vermin?

John: You've got it. And by the way, this is how conversion relates directly to those social issues you mentioned in the beginning of our conversation. Conversion is personal, like you said, but it's never private. It always relates to persons and their society.

Rick: This is the same kind of love you've talked about before in your sermons. What do you call it? *Agape* love, was it?

John: Right. It is the love of the will. Jesus Christ had to will to love those who slew him. And we dare not say that he pulled rank on us and was other than man! He was man on that Cross. Gods don't die. He died.

Rick: I've always wondered about that. I've asked a hundred times if he really hurt like I do.

John: He did. And he had the same frightened, ashamed feelings you and I would have had we been up there. Stripped naked before enemies, pummeled with insults, pierced with weapons, exposed with no defense except his love. What if this had been you and me? What would we have said?

Rick: I'd let 'em know they'd been in a fight. I'd have taken one with me!

John: Probably most of us would. We would have been like Simon Peter who drew his sword and cut off an enemy's ear. Simon had not learned to live like Jesus yet. He was being converted to his principles and way, his truth and life, but not yet. Tradition has it that Simon was crucified later, too. He died like Jesus, but only after he had learned to live like Jesus.

Rick: Died crucified upside down, didn't he?

John: Tradition says so. You know, Rick, the way a man lives and the way he dies fit together. Jesus died like he lived: with *agape*.

Rick: For the first time in my life conversion sounds real and exciting. It can stand on its own two feet, then! This kind of conversion can even handle its enemies!

John: No doubt about it. When we die to the old self, then we can live like the Master. Let our enemies come. Let them strip us of dignity and we can still love them. Let them disappoint us and we can still embrace them. Let them squander our most cherished beliefs and we can still accept them. Let them slander us and we can still pray redemptively for them. Let them take our lives and we shall not fear.

Rick: It's beginning to fall into place. All those old Sunday school lessons and sermons, I mean. You can't kill his kind of love. His enemies thought they had. But what you're saying is that his kind of love is not buried in rock walls or covered over by common soil, or wrapped forever in burial clothes.

John: Right! His kind of love always lives. It always has and it always will. And when we know true conversion, then we share in the victory of an inconquerable love—*agape*. That's what conversion is all about.

Rick: This is a religion where Christ really is Master, isn't it? I must go now. Thanks for your time, John. I've got a brainful of things to consider. Maybe this conversion *is* needed more than I saw before. Good-by, John. And thanks.

You know what I prayed one night, dad? It was a crazy kid's prayer. I prayed that God would make another day in the week so that you would have enough time to spend with me. Can you imagine that? But then I grew too old to cry. Yet the desire to have you home and close to me was still there, like when I was a little kid. But I couldn't cry, so I raised hell at school. The hell that was inside me, dad, it came out. It had to or I would have burst inside. It just spilled out all over everything and everybody. I couldn't help it. It just came out.—The son

"I'll Tell You, Dad"...
"I'll Tell You, Son"

Children, it is your Christian duty to obey your parents, for this is the right thing to do.

Parents, do not treat your children in such a way as to make them angry. Instead, raise them with Christian discipline and instruction.—*Ephesians 6:1,4*

Dad: Congratulations, son. Your mom and I were so pleased to hear that you and Jane have a new baby boy. That's great. I had just finished reading the paper when you rang the doorbell. Come on in the house and sit with me. Mom's just left for the store. Sit down, sit down—I'll fix us a coke.

Son: Thanks, dad. Jane's doing fine and we're real pleased with our first-born. Just think, a boy! I can hardly believe it.

Dad: That's what you were, son, our first-born. And a boy! [*Chuckling.*] But I guess you know that by now! Here's your coke, son. Sit down. Relax. Well, I hope you have as happy a home as we had, son! You and Sissy and mom and me. Yes sir, we had quite a life together. What about that boy? Don't you hope your home is as happy as ours?

Son: Uh, well—Yeah, dad. I guess so.

Dad: Well, you don't sound too convincing. Is everything all right, son? Jane and the boy are all right, aren't they? You said—

Son: Yeah, yeah—everything's great, dad. Just great.

Dad: Well, you're probably just worried about being a dad, a father. Don't worry about it, son, there's not much to it. Take it from me, there's really not much to being a parent. You just sorta move with them, stay young at heart, and all that. [*Laughs.*]

Son: That's what I'm worried about, dad. I'm not sure that's all there is to it. I've had to do some hard thinking about being a father.

Dad: Well, that's all your mom and I did. It'll turn out okay. You'll see. After all, I was a pretty good "old man," wasn't I?

Son: You were fair, dad.

Dad: Fair, just fair? [*Pause.*] Hey, wait a minute. Are you trying to tell me something, boy? Are you trying to tell me something about the way mom and I raised you and Sissy?

Son: Maybe I am, dad. It's not that you didn't try, or that you didn't want to do what's right, but—well—you and mom missed a lot. Jane and I don't want to miss those things with our kids. We want things to be different.

Dad: [*Defensively.*] Now, wait just a minute, boy. Your mom and I did a lot for you and Sissy. You aren't forgetting that, are you? Huh? I mean, we may have made some mistakes and all, but we did our best. And like they say, "That's all a man can do." His best!

Son: I'm sure you thought you did. You tried. But it could have been better. You and mom just plain missed the boat sometimes.

Dad: Missed the boat? Well, how's that for ingratitude? I've taught you better than that, boy—

Son: Don't call me boy, will you? I feel like a black servant when you do that.

Dad: Well, I'll tell you, you're really on your high horse, aren't you? But, son, you know what I think? I think you're an ingrate. After all I've done for you. Why, your mother and I gave up a lot of things for you. We wanted things, we needed things sometimes, but no, we couldn't have them because you and Sissy needed them, too. And now you talk that way about your mother and me? That leaves a bitter taste, son, a real bitter taste.

Son: Well, I've got some bitterness, too, dad. You talk about how much you gave me and Sissy, how much you sacrificed, how you worked your fingers to the bone for me. You just never did really understand—you and mom. You never realized that Sissy and I owed you nothing.

Dad: Owed us nothing? We give you life, health, a good home, you eat our food for eighteen years. And you owe us nothing?

Son: I don't owe you a thing, dad, not a thing. You and mom— all parents—bring your children into the world and if you're responsible, if you care, you do what's necessary for them.

Dad: No thanks at all, eh?

Son: No, dad. I'm saying that you do what you have to do, and not just for them but for yourselves, too. You couldn't live with the guilt if you didn't do what you had to do! So don't blame me for being born. You brought me into this world. I didn't ask you to come, and you as a responsible person had to care for me when I got here.

Dad: That's all there is to it, huh? Just as cut-and-dried as all that? I like to think that there was some appreciation for the sacrifice that we—

Son: [*Interrupts.*] Don't start now with that sacrifice bit. If you did sacrifice, it's because you had to take care of what you had conceived. You may not like it, dad, but this is the way I feel. You'll never know how guilty and bad you used to make me and Sissy feel when you talked about all those "sacrifices" you made. We felt terrible. We wished at times we'd never been born. Sissy and I thought we had brought something to the family, not taken away from it.

Dad: You ought to at least respect us for bringing you into the world.

Son: No! I'm grateful for you and mom giving me physical birth, but you have to earn respect, dad. I feel that there's more to being a parent than the natural production of children. There's time and understanding, and patience and God knows what all. And honesty. Man, this world—this sick old world—needs a hefty dose of honesty. [*Sighs.*] Well those are my feelings, dad.

Dad: So, I guess the next thing you're going to say is that this is the reason you couldn't stay out of trouble at school? All this modern psychology says you get in trouble to call attention to your problems. I don't believe all that—

Son: I would have been better off if you had believed it, if you had listened. Just a little.

Dad: Now, wait a minute. I used to listen to you.

Son: Yeah, through a newspaper or while you gobbled down your supper or in a casual, "Yeah, yeah," as you rushed out the door to go to a meeting of some sort. You went through the motions but you never really listened!

Dad: Well, you didn't listen to me either. Why didn't you listen to me, boy—son? I can remember the times when I would advise you and you would just sneer at me. You didn't listen either!

Son: You want to know why? Because a lot of mothers and fathers just like you and mom have a cockeyed way of looking at the world. You don't play the game fair, dad. I heard some guy singing a song on the radio, and he said something about, "If the mind is baffled when the rules don't fit the game, who will answer?" That's what I want to know, too. You cheated, dad.

Dad: Cheated? Why, I've never—

Son: Don't do yourself the harm of lying, dad. How did you expect me to take you seriously when you told me not to fight at school and you slapped me around at home?

Dad: That was my right as your father!

Son: But I'm telling you my feelings now. I'm not talking about rights, unless you don't care to hear any more—

Dad: No. [*Pauses.*] I'll listen to what you have to say. I thought I was doing the right thing. To try to discipline you, I mean. I may have whipped a little hard, but—

Son: But every time you took your belt off to whip me you know what you were teaching me? You were teaching me that there's only one real answer to a problem and that's violence. Hit! Hit! Hit! And you used to give me those little sex lectures on keeping myself pure with the girls and all that, but I know that on those business trips to Chicago you—

Dad: Son! How did you know—?

Son: Don't ask me how I knew. I just did. You talked a good game of honesty. But one day I opened the glove compartment of your car and there were a dozen crumpled, yellowed police tickets for as many violations.

Dad: So I made mistakes. None of us is perfect. You'll find that out as a father. Every man makes mistakes.

Son: I could understand how you would make mistakes. But you never stood responsible for them, dad. And somehow that two-word lecture in morality you used to give hung up in my brain. "Be straight. Be straight!" What you said and the way you lived didn't go together, dad.

Dad: Well, just go ahead. Tell me everything I ever did wrong. Lay me low, son! No, I'm serious, don't shake your head like that. Tell me where mom and I went wrong.

Son: I don't want to hurt you, dad. But there are some things I need to say. I've never said them before, but I'm a father now. I've become a man. I need to tell you those things as a man. [*Pauses.*] Time was the big thing, dad.

Dad: Time?

Son: Yes, time. You see, the way I look at it, time means love. You spend some time with a person and that means you care for that person; it means you love him. At least, this is what I learned in the church. That's true for everyone, but especially for kids. Dad, you were long on lectures, but short on time. I remember I used to lie in my bed at night and wish you would come home and walk in and sit down on my bed and talk with me. I cried myself to sleep at night wishing you had more time.

Dad: There were some kids whose dads didn't work. They had plenty of time but no bed for their kids to sleep in. I just didn't know you felt that way.

113

Son: I did. I felt it deeply. You know what I prayed one night, dad? It was a crazy kid's prayer. I prayed that God would make another day in the week so that you would have enough time to spend with me. Can you imagine that? But then I grew too old to cry. Yet the desire to have you home and close to me was still there, like when I was a little kid. But I couldn't cry, so I raised hell at school. The hell that was inside me, dad, it came out. It had to or I would have burst inside. It just spilled out all over everything and everybody. I couldn't help it. It just came out.

Dad: You'll never know how frustrating this is. I've worked my fingers to the bone to keep body and soul together. You wanted to work but you were good in sports so I took an extra job to let you run track. Now you tell me—

Son: [*Interrupts.*] And do you know why I was so good in sports in high school? I was playing for you, dad. But you were never there. You never cared enough to come watch me perform. I was good in track. I wasn't the best, but I did my best. But it was nothing, do you hear—*nothing*— because there was no one there to meet me at the finish line! Oh, there were a thousand people there, but *you* weren't there, so nobody was there. I ran my guts out for you. But you weren't there.

Dad: But, son, I had to work. I had to put food on the table. Bread and beans and meat.

Son: Oh, for God's sake, dad. When is a bowl of beans more important than a person? We could have done without the beans, or even the meat. You could have taken one day off! I needed your time, dad. We'll always have beans. Some farmer will always grow us some beans, but that time with me is gone! All the money in the world can't buy that back.

Dad: But mom and I had our problems, son. Maybe that's why I didn't give you and Sissy more time.

Son: I know. Sissy and I used to hear you around the breakfast table. We knew. But I don't think you ever understood mom, either. You had problems, sure, but you could've gotten help. If you had just swallowed some of that pride you could have been happier people. Sissy and

114

I could have been happier, too. You always had a difficult time admitting that you were wrong.

Dad: I find it hard to believe that you have said these things to me. If I had known—

Son: You could have known it, if you had asked me.

Dad: And to think you were so active in church and still feel this way?

Son: It was the church that taught me to be honest. It was the church that accepted my true feelings, that loved me through it all. You would have been better off if you had been more involved. But no! You got your feelings hurt and withdrew like a frightened turtle draws up in his shell.

Dad: But they didn't treat me right. They hurt me down there at that church. I swore I'd never go back. I was justified in my decision.

Son: Maybe so, I can't judge that. But I can say that it would have been better for us all—me, Sissy, you and mom—if you had gone with me to church instead of dropping me on its doorstep every Sunday like a sack of mail at a railroad station. That hurt, too, dad. I found something good and strong, something solid as gold in that church.

Dad: Bah! Bunch of hypocrites. Talk religion and live like sin itself!

Son: Sure those people have their faults—they had a lot of them. But you know where they were one up on you, dad?

Dad: Where? Yes, I'd like to know. Where were they one up on me?

Son: They had those faults forgiven. And when you really think about it, it's not having faults that matters, it's getting them healed, forgiven, having someone to understand them that counts. You know the difference between making mistakes and being a failure? The difference is forgiveness.

Dad: That's what you're giving me now, huh? You call what you've said forgiveness?

Son: I had to get it out, dad. I can tell you because I have forgiven you. I needed to clean out my soul. But I forgive you. I really do. I've been forgiving you for a long time. I

252.0617
C7521

130 534

guess— It's just that—well, this is the last step, I guess.

Dad: You really mean that?

Son: Sure. I just don't want you to be a bitter old man, that's all. I don't ever want to find you sitting out on the front porch nursing all the grievances and hurts of life, keeping them alive and sucking all the bitter venom from them.

Dad: Is there any good that I've done? No plus marks on the ledger of our relationship?

Son: A lot, dad. But even more for the future. If it helps, think of it this way. I've learned from your mistakes. I've got a son, now, a child of clay that's waiting to be shaped, molded in life. And maybe I can be a better father to him than you were to me. That's something, isn't it? At least it doesn't just add up to zero.

Dad: It makes some sense. I don't guess you *could* have told me all that if you hadn't forgiven me, could you? [*Smiles.*] That's one thing in my favor.

Son: What's that?

Dad: I've raised a son who can forgive. That's something.

Son: Can I make a suggestion, dad?

Dad: Sure, son.

Son: Get back in the church now. It's not too late. It's the faith of the church that lets you see your mistakes with forgiveness and hope. And that's really something, too, dad. It truly is. That's why I'm learning from our mistakes together. I have hope for my new boy. Take the church and its lord and let him really become yours. And you, his.

Dad: It's awfully late, son. I'm a grandfather now. There are a lot of years to account for.

Son: It doesn't matter. About the time and years, I mean. Let him have you, remold you, remake you, forgive you, reconcile you to your enemies. Age doesn't make any difference. He can do it with anyone. All he needs is a willing spirit. He's helped me and he'll be with me as I try to be a good father to that new son of mine. I'll tell you, dad, he can make all the difference in the world.

Dad: I'll tell you, son—you just may be right. Wouldn't that be something?

3 4711 00225 4441